1780:
Year of Revenge

JOHN L. MOORE

Mechanicsburg, PA USA

Published by Sunbury Press, Inc.
Mechanicsburg, Pennsylvania

www.sunburypress.com

Copyright © 2019 by John L. Moore.
Cover Copyright © 2019 by Sunbury Press, Inc.

Sunbury Press supports copyright. Copyright fuels creativity, encourages diverse voices, promotes free speech, and creates a vibrant culture. Thank you for buying an authorized edition of this book and for complying with copyright laws by not reproducing, scanning, or distributing any part of it in any form without permission. You are supporting writers and allowing Sunbury Press to continue to publish books for every reader. For information contact Sunbury Press, Inc., Subsidiary Rights Dept., PO Box 548, Boiling Springs, PA 17007 USA or legal@sunburypress.com.

For information about special discounts for bulk purchases, please contact Sunbury Press Orders Dept. at (855) 338-8359 or orders@sunburypress.com.

To request one of our authors for speaking engagements or book signings, please contact Sunbury Press Publicity Dept. at publicity@sunburypress.com.

ISBN: 978-1-62006-179-4 (Trade paperback)

Library of Congress Control Number: Application in Process

FIRST SUNBURY PRESS EDITION: May 2019

Product of the United States of America
0 1 1 2 3 5 8 13 21 34 55

Set in Bookman Old Style
Designed by Crystal Devine
Cover by Lawrence Knorr
Cover art by Andrew Knez Jr.
Edited by Lawrence Knorr

Continue the Enlightenment!

In Memory of two professors who encouraged and inspired their students

Walter M. Brasch, Bloomsburg University, Bloomsburg, Pa.

and

Gerhard D. Zeller, Moravian College, Bethlehem, Pa., and SUNY Oswego, N.Y.

Contents

Acknowledgments vii
Author's Note viii

Prologue: 'Why aren't the Iroquois
suing for peace?' 1

November 1777: Hardly a day without
'some new murder' 6

The New Purchase of 1768 attracts
hundreds of homesteaders 15

December 1776: Riflemen, scouts
leave Sunbury for the battlefields of
New Jersey 19

June 1, 1779: Sullivan's army gathers
at Easton 28

May 1778: Indian raids terrorize the
Susquehanna Valley 22

July 1778: Continental troops arrive
to defend the West Branch Valley 27

Hawkins Boone fortifies his mill on
Muddy Run 31

November 1779: The German Regiment
stationed at Susquehanna forts 39

January 1780: Iroquois warriors
shiver, starve, plot revenge 45

March 29: The capture of Lieutenant
Moses Van Campen 51

Ferocious firefight erupts along the
upper Delaware.......................57

April 25: Raiders torch Gilbert's mills,
take 15 captives 59

William Maclay's appeal: 'Help us
if you can'...........................68

Pennsylvania offers a reward for scalps
of Indians 75

War parties employ hit-and-run tactics
in raiding settlements 78

'I do not find that they ever stir a foot
out of their posts' 83

Mid-summer 1780: The German
Regiment marches away 92

Fort Augusta soldiers seize boats
shipping flour to Wyoming............103

Epilogue 110

Bibliography 112
About the author...................113

Acknowledgments

Jane P. Moore and Robert B. Swift read the manuscript and suggested improvements that have made *1780: Year of Revenge* a better book.

Author's Note

The people whose experiences are chronicled in this book died centuries ago. Their stories survive in letters, diaries, journals, official reports, depositions, interrogations, examinations, minutes and memoirs. These are quoted liberally. An occasional ellipsis (. . .) indicates where words or phrases have been omitted. Punctuation and spelling have been modernized.

Throughout 1780, Joseph Reed, a Philadelphia lawyer, served as president of Pennsylvania's Supreme Executive Council. Many people, especially officers of the Pennsylvania Militia, referred to him as President Reed. Reed's responsibilities as president made him the state's de facto governor, and many others, George Washington among them, addressed him as Governor Reed. To avoid confusion, the text refers to Reed as governor. The text occasionally refers to two other men–Thomas Wharton, Jr., and George Bryan–who also served as president of Pennsylvania's Supreme Executive Council. They are also referred to as governor.

PROLOGUE

'Why aren't the Iroquois suing for peace?'

The story of 1780, by all accounts a year of bloody revenge on the Pennsylvania frontier, begins in April 1775 with the opening shots of the American Revolutionary War in the Massachusetts villages of Lexington and Concord.

The war had a huge impact on the Iroquois Indians. When it started, the Six Nations of the Iroquois Confederacy—also known as The Haudenosaunee, which translates as People of the Longhouse—occupied much of the land that has since become western New York State. West of the Hudson River were the Mohawks, who tended the eastern door of the Iroquois' metaphorical longhouse. In turn, the Senecas guarded its western door, which was in the region of the Niagara River. The four other nations—the Oneidas, Tuscaroras, Onondagas, and Cayugas—occupied the land in between.

At first, the Iroquois attempted to avoid taking sides with either the British or the rebellious Americans, but as the war heated up, beginning in August 1777 and throughout 1778, war parties of Senecas and other western Iroquois repeatedly raided frontier settlements in Pennsylvania, New Jersey, and New York. The warriors obtained weapons, ammunition, and other supplies from British soldiers at Fort

Iroquois war parties met in this Seneca Council House along the Genesee River in western New York and planned raids against Pennsylvania frontier settlements. It has been restored and moved to Letchworth State Park, New York.

Niagara, an outpost on Lake Ontario, or from Fort Detroit, a British post near the western end of Lake Erie, before they set out for the American settlements. When they returned, they sold the scalps of frontier settlers to the British. At Detroit, Lieutenant Colonel Henry Hamilton purchased so many American scalps from returning war parties that he acquired a nickname, The Hair Buyer.

In early 1779, General George Washington decided to retaliate against the Indians who had joined the British. He sent a Continental Army led by Major General John Sullivan across eastern Pennsylvania, up the Susquehanna River, and into western New York. He also dispatched a smaller force commanded by Colonel Daniel Brodhead at Fort Pitt in western Pennsylvania up the Allegheny River. Both armies sought out native towns and destroyed them. Washington regarded this initiative as a "rod of correction" that punished tribes that had warred against the United States.

Brodhead subsequently reported that his 600 soldiers had destroyed eleven towns and related farms along the Allegheny. In some villages, "the Indian houses were . . . built of square and round logs and frame work," the colonel said

George Washington

in a September 16 letter to Washington. He added that "the quantity of corn and other vegetables destroyed . . . from the best accounts I can collect from the officers employed to destroy it must certainly exceed 500 acres."

In turn, Sullivan informed Washington that his 4,000 men had penetrated deep into the Iroquois homeland and laid it waste. "There is not a single town left in the country of the Five *(sic)* Nations," Sullivan said in his report, dated September 28.

The Indians had mounted little opposition as Sullivan's soldiers advanced. They had fought and lost one battle early in Sullivan's invasion. After that, as the Americans slowly moved into Iroquois homeland, entire villages and towns withdrew to Fort Niagara, which stood at the mouth of the Niagara River on the western end of Lake Ontario. Before the Continentals returned to Pennsylvania, they burned 41 native towns and wrecked all the Indian farms they encountered. Sullivan reported to Washington that his men had destroyed more than 160,000 bushels of maize.

Although the Americans left the Iroquois country without attacking Fort Niagara, Sullivan assured his commander that "there is not at this time even the appearance of an Indian on this side (of) the Genesee (River), and I believe there is not one on this side (of) Niagara, nor is there any kind of sustenance left for them in this country."

The Sullivan and Brodhead reports greatly pleased Washington, who told the Marquis de Lafayette on October 20 that Sullivan "has completed the entire destruction of the country of the Six Nations (and) driven all the inhabitants—men, women, and children—out of it."

Colonel Samuel Hunter, who died in 1784, was buried in a small cemetery adjacent to Fort Augusta in Sunbury, Pa. Hunter commanded the Northumberland County Militia throughout the American Revolution.

Washington persuaded himself that the destruction wrought by Sullivan and Brodhead had shown the Iroquois the danger of continuing as British allies and convinced them to sit out the war. "These unexpected and severe strokes has (sic) disconcerted, humbled, and distressed the Indians exceedingly, and will, I am persuaded, be productive of great good. . . . They are undeniable proofs to them that Great Britain cannot protect them, and that it is in our power to chastise them whenever their hostile conduct deserves it."

Not every American shared Washington's assessment. In Pennsylvania, Colonel Samuel Hunter, the commander at Fort Augusta on the Susquehanna River at Sunbury, had paid close attention to the progress of Sullivan's campaign. As the officer in charge of the Northumberland County Militia, Hunter had the responsibility for protecting a large section of the frontier north of Sunbury. Earlier in the year, Seneca war parties had terrorized Hunter's region even as Sullivan organized his invasion force 70 miles upriver at Wilkes-Barre.

Two months after Sullivan's return to the eastern front, Hunter remained at his frontier post and fretted about the future. Writing to Governor Joseph Reed from Sunbury on November 27, Hunter remarked that it "seems very strange" that "there is no account of any Indians coming from the northward to sue for peace in the distressed condition . . . they must be in." The absence of such news "makes me afraid they are meditating something cruel against our frontier counties early in the next spring, but I trust in God it may not be the case," Hunter said.

The events of 1780 not only show the accuracy of Hunter's interpretation of events, but also the magnitude of Washington's mistake in misjudging the consequences of Sullivan's strategy.

Chapter 1

November 1777: Hardly a day without 'some new murder'

When the Revolution began, the Iroquois regarded it as a conflict between a powerful but distant father and his rebellious son. They saw little reason to take sides, at least in the beginning.

Indeed, in July 1775 the Continental Congress formally asked the Iroquois to be neutral. "This is a family quarrel between us and Old England," the Congress said. "You Indians are not concerned in it. We don't wish you to take up the hatchet against the king's troops. We desire you to remain at home, and not join on either side, but keep the hatchet buried deep."

In Pittsburgh a year later, American military officers held a formal meeting at Fort Pitt with Kiashuta, the Six Nations representative, or Half King, in the Ohio River Valley. Important chiefs of the Delawares and Shawnees also attended. Kiashuta expressed the Iroquois position bluntly: "We will not suffer either the English or Americans to march an army through our country."

The half-king referred to the nearly 300-mile expanse of territory that lay between Fort Pitt and the British post at Fort Detroit near the western end of Lake Erie. Emphasizing that the Six Nations had made him responsible for "the care of the Indians on

Joseph Brant, Mohawk warrior

the west side of the River Ohio," Kiashuta urged the Americans to abandon any plans they had to stage "an expedition against Detroit, for I repeat it to you again, we will not suffer an army to march through our country."

The Iroquois leader explained that the Six Nations wanted no part in the war. They had sent a belt of wampum to the Delawares, Shawnees, and other western tribes and urged them to stay out of the fight.

Despite Kiashuta's statement, which he made on July 6, 1776, any chance that the Indians had of remaining neutral had already splintered. As early as April 1775, the Americans fighting at Boston in April 1775 had welcomed Stockbridge Indians from western Massachusetts into their ranks. The presence of these native warriors helped erode any reluctance that British officers may have had about recruiting Indians to fight for King George III. "The rebels themselves have opened the door," remarked General Thomas Gage, the British commander, in September 1775. "They have brought down all they could against us here."

Soon after this, George III appointed Lord George Germain as Secretary of State for North America, an appointment that made Germain responsible for planning and prosecuting the war against the rebellious colonies. In 1776, the London-based Germain instructed two of his top generals, William Howe in New York and John Burgoyne in Canada, to send Indian war parties against the colonies' western frontiers.

In the spring of 1776, as General Burgoyne prepared to depart England for Quebec, Germain told him that "the assistance of the Indians . . . would be highly necessary, and that their tempers and dispositions were to be cultivated with particular attention." The minister followed up in an August 23 letter: "The dread the people of New England etc. have of a war with the savages proves the expediency of our holding that scourge over them."

In a March 28, 1776 letter to General Howe, Germain said that ". . . securing the assistance of the Indians was an important consideration."

Despite Germain's directives, Howe and Burgoyne, who employed conventional military tactics, weren't especially eager to employ native warriors as adjuncts to British regulars. At the same time, many Americans still hoped that the Indians would stay on the sidelines.

When an American officer, Major General Philip Schuyler, invited the Iroquois to a mid-summer peace treaty to be held at German Flatts *(sic)* on the Mohawk River in western New York, more than 1,700

Iroquois turned out. According to Schuyler, this figure included "their women and children." One of the women was Mary Jemison, the wife of an influential war chief Hiakatoo. An adopted Seneca, she had been abducted from her family's Pennsylvania farm during the French and Indian War two decades earlier.

"The Six Nations solemnly agreed that if a war should eventually break out, they would not take up arms on either side; but that they would observe a strict neutrality," Jemison later told her biographer, James Seaver.

The German Flatts conference ended in early August 1776, and General Schuyler told Washington, "I believe the Six Nations will not fall on our frontiers, although I believe a few will always join the enemy in Canada." For her part, Mary Jemison recalled, "The Indians returned to their homes well pleased that they could live on neutral ground, surrounded by the din of war, without being engaged in it."

Nearly six months later, in late January 1777, the Continental Congress and the Pennsylvania Council of Safety sent delegates to Easton for an unofficial treaty requested by the Six Nations. Some 70 Iroquois leaders traveled hundreds of miles from western New York to attend the conference, described in the January 20 minutes of the Council of Safety as intended "to preserve peace and harmony with the Indian nations."

Colonel George Taylor, a member of the Continental Congress, presided over the meeting. "If they are to be relied on, they mean to be neuter (neutral)," reported Colonel John Bull, a member of the Council of Safety and a Pennsylvania delegate to the treaty.

As the conference ended, the council shipped an assortment of goods to Easton for Bull to hand out as gifts. These included 9,600 white wampum beads and 20,500 black wampum beads, and decorative jewelry that included 30 moons and 30 hair pipes of conk shell, six pair (of) armbands, 100 broaches, 37 pair (of) ear bobs, all of silver. Fifteen camp kettles were also distributed.

In early 1777, some western Pennsylvanians even saw merit in providing Indians with ammunition for their firearms. On April 18, 1777, for instance, officials of the Westmoreland County Committee wrote to Colonel George Morgan, the Indian Affairs Agent at Pittsburgh, and said they were aware of "the Delawares' applying to you for powder and lead." Based in Hannastown, the Westmoreland County seat some 30 miles east of Pittsburgh, the committee favored "every measure that can be taken to preserve the peace with any tribe or nations of Indians on whose friendship we can depend, and we are of opinion that it would be advisable to supply them (the Delaware) with ammunition," according to Samuel Sloan and James Hamilton, the committee members who signed the letter.

As it happened, Iroquois neutrality didn't last the summer of 1777. An August 6 battle in New York's Mohawk River Valley saw Seneca and Mohawk warriors siding with the Loyalists, and Oneida warriors allied with the Americans. The fighting started when a force of Loyalists and Indians ambushed a column of New York militia accompanied by Oneida warriors in a ravine near Oriskany Creek about eight miles from Fort Stanwix (present-day Rome, New York.) The Loyalists and Indians routed the New Yorkers, and one Tory estimated that 500 Americans were wounded or killed.

Around this time, war parties supplied by British officers at Fort Niagara on Lake Ontario and Fort Detroit began raiding the frontier. By late summer, "Indian ravages" had become so severe in western Pennsylvania that Lieutenant Colonel Archibald

Lochry of the Westmoreland County militia appealed to the Council of Safety for "all the rifled guns, of which that county is very bare, that may be had." Settlers in that county also needed ammunition so they could "make some defense at their habitations, and at large," Thomas Wharton, president of Pennsylvania's Supreme Executive Council, informed John Hancock, then president of the Continental Congress. The Westmoreland settlements lay 30 miles west of the Allegheny Mountains. In his September 8 letter to Hancock, Wharton predicted that "without something be(ing) done for their relief, the Allegheny Mountain will soon become the frontier."

Two days later and 150 miles to the east, Colonel Hunter at Fort Augusta reported that a rumor had swept Northumberland County's northern settlements that a force of 200 Indians was "coming down upon our frontiers." Reacting to the rumor, "a colonel of our militia, one Cookson Long, set off last Saturday with a party of men to know if they had any hostile intentions," Hunter said in a September 10 letter. ". . . I hope the report he brings back may be favorable, as we are badly off in this county for want of arms and ammunition."

In early October, residents of Ligonier, a settlement along Loyalhanna Creek about 50 miles southeast of Pittsburgh, felt sufficiently threatened that they constructed a stockade fort. Some men dug a trench in which to erect the log palisades, and others began felling trees and trimming them into logs for the stockade wall.

Work on the fort was well along when at 2 p.m. on the afternoon of October 13, an express rider arrived from Colonel Lochry. He and a detachment of 15 men were escorting a west-bound pack train of 140 horses carrying military supplies. They had reached the ford where the Bedford-Pittsburgh road crossed

In October 1777, settlers at Hannastown in western Pennsylvania erected a stockade fort as a place of retreat in the event of an Indian attack. The structure in the photograph is a replica in the recreated village site of Historic Hanna's Town, which is operated by the Westmoreland Historical Society.

Stony Creek, about 19 miles east of Ligonier. The colonel suspected that hostile Indians were waiting to ambush the pack train near the crossing. "A man had been killed and scalped the day before within half a mile of that place," the express rider reported. Lochry had halted the column at the ford and wanted reinforcements from Ligonier before continuing west.

At daybreak on October 14, "Captain Shannon with 24 men marched to Stony Creek to his relief," according to a journal kept by an anonymous Ligonier man. Shannon's departure stopped work on the fort temporarily, "there being only a guard for the town left."

The pack train came into Ligonier at about 4 o'clock in the afternoon "without any accident on the road," the journal said.

Indian raids continued throughout the fall. The mounting casualties in Westmoreland County included "eleven . . . persons killed and scalped at Palmers Fort near Ligonier," Colonel Lochry reported in early November.

A street scene in the recreated village site of Historic Hanna's Town, which is operated by the Westmoreland Historical Society.

Following one attack, Westmoreland frontiersmen had found a proclamation "left by the savages from the governor of Detroit requesting all persons to come to him, or any other of the garrisons occupied by His Majesty's troops, and they should receive pay and lodgings as they rank with us," Lochry reported. Also, civilians who came in would be given 200 acres of land.

Westmoreland inhabitants had also erected a second stockade fort, this one at Hannastown, also "at the public expense," Lochry reported on November 4. Each post contained "a storehouse . . . to secure both public and private property . . . and be a place of retreat for the suffering frontiers in case of necessity."

At Fort Augusta on October 27, Colonel Hunter reported receiving a shipment of ammunition—"500 pounds of powder and 1,200 pounds of lead"—but no rifled guns, which are "much wanted in this county, for in case the Indians commences (*sic*) hostilities, we are badly off for arms." In a report to Governor Wharton, Hunter said, "Colonel John Kelly . . . is out at this present time with a party of 50 men and an

Indian called Job Chillaway to reconnoiter and make discoveries of any enemy Indians . . . within 50 miles of the Great Island (present-day Lock Haven)." Should Kelly fail to find a sign of hostiles, "it will be a means of encouraging the poor settlers to go back to their respective habitations. . . . upwards of 500 of men, women, and children (are) assembled at three different places on the West Branch of Susquehanna, Viz. at the mouth of Bald Eagle (Lock Haven), Antes's Mill (near Jersey Shore) and Lycoming (Williamsport). There is some friend(ly) Indians with their families come in to our people whom I allow provisions while they stay."

Major General John Sullivan

In Bedford County, "an Indian war is now raging around us in its utmost fury," Thomas Smith and George Woods told the governor on November 27. Raids had become so commonplace that, "in short, a day hardly passes without our hearing of some new murder," they wrote.

Chapter 2

The New Purchase of 1768 attracts hundreds of homesteaders

The upper branches of the Susquehanna River drain a wide, almost funnel-shaped section of Central and Northeastern Pennsylvania. As the crow flies, Lock Haven on the West Branch is nearly 90 miles west of Wilkes-Barre on the North Branch. The city sits nearly 60 miles northwest of Northumberland, where the West Branch joins the North Branch to form the Susquehanna's main stem. In turn, Wilkes-Barre's location on the North Branch is nearly 70 miles above the confluence.

At the Susquehanna's confluence, the West and North Branches form a wide but shallow river that flows mostly south before shifting ever so slightly to the southeast and emptying into the Chesapeake Bay about 130 miles below the confluence.

During the 1670s, the Iroquois had acquired ownership—but not necessarily taken possession in the European sense—of this entire region by right of conquest over the Susquehannocks, a warlike people that lived in palisaded towns along the lower river. As English immigrants established the Pennsylvania colony during the 1680s, the Europeans at first concentrated their farms and villages along the Delaware and Schuylkill rivers—far to the east of the Susquehanna.

When the French and Indian War began in 1755, nearly all the people living north of present-day Harrisburg in this region were Native Americans. There were numerous Indian towns along the Susquehanna, notably Shamokin at present-day Sunbury; Nescopeck and Wyoming (Wilkes-Barre) on the North Branch; and Otzinachson (Montoursville) and Great Island (Lock Haven) on the West Branch. Other than fur traders and missionaries, few people of European descent lived in the territory. To be certain, some white settlers had ventured west of the Susquehanna to establish farms, but these people were few.

The next 20 years saw a tremendous shift in the region's population, especially after 1768, when the Iroquois sold a vast expanse of land to the British. This immense territory sprawled across the western frontiers of New York, Pennsylvania, and Virginia. The sale occurred during a treaty at Fort Stanwix, a British outpost more than 100 miles northwest of Albany, New York.

Pennsylvania referred to its share of this territory as the New Purchase of 1768. The colony acquired heavily forested regions along both sides of the Susquehanna's North Branch, along the entire length of the southern side of the West Branch, and along parts of the Allegheny and Monongahela rivers.

White settlers soon swarmed into the upper Susquehanna Valley. Within four years two new settlements at the forks—Sunbury and Northumberland—had become sufficiently populous for the colonial government to formally recognize them as towns. The same year—1772—the colony organized Northumberland County with Sunbury as the county seat.

Nearly all the Indians had left the Susquehanna Valley by then. The Rev. Phillip Vickers Fithian, a Presbyterian circuit rider who traveled on horseback along the West Branch during the summer of 1775, hardly encountered any natives at all. After leaving Northumberland, he traveled a full 70 miles upriver before seeing any. The clergyman had reached Lock Haven, then a village just across the West Branch from unsold Iroquois territory, when, on July 26, "I saw today two Indians! Young fellows about 18." They were taking their furs downriver to trade, and "they had neat, clean rifles."

As white people moved into the New Purchase, they set about clearing forests for farmland, building log cabins and barns, digging millraces to power newly-built gristmills, widening and improving native trails for use by horse- and ox-drawn wagons, and erecting churches for fledgling congregations. As homesteaders established farms along the river, river men quickly built boats and began shipping farm goods to downriver markets and mills.

Fithian documented much of this as he rode through the region in June and July 1775. Of Sunbury, the preacher wrote on June 27, "It is yet a small village, but seems to be growing rapidly," Following a visit on July 19, he added, "It may contain 100 houses. All the buildings are of logs but Mr. (William) McClay's, which is of stone, and large and elegant."

Across the Susquehanna stood Northumberland. "Here are a number of boatmen employed in going up and down the river to Middletown. With these and others from the country this infant village seems busy and noisy as a Philadelphia ferry-house," Fithian said.

At Warriors Run—present-day Watsontown—on Sunday, July 16, along the West Branch 18 miles north of Northumberland, carpenters hadn't yet put a roof on the congregation's new church, so "I preached from a wagon," Fithian said. Lacking pews, "the people sat on a rising ground before me." They paid close attention to his sermon. Even so, Fithian thought it "looks odd to see the people sitting among the bushes."

The influx of would-be homesteaders showed little sign of slowing even seven years after the purchase. Writing from Northumberland on July 19, Fithian reported, "two wagons, with goods, cattle, women, tools, etc., went through town today from East Jersey, on their way to Fishing Creek up this river, where they are to settle. Rapid, most rapid, is the growth of this county."

As Fithian traveled up the West Branch, he went along the river's east shore. "All this way is a good wagon-beaten road," he wrote. At Muncy, the West Branch swung abruptly to the west and went past the present-day communities of Williamsport, Jersey Shore, and Lock Haven.

The Six Nations continued to own the land northwest of Jersey Shore, and Fithian wrote that when he reached the "Indian's land" across from the New Purchase, the road soon became "a narrow path."

Above the Great Island at Lock Haven—"I call it 70 miles from Sunbury."—the clergyman encountered a prosperous landowner named Fleming. "Mr. Fleming tells me this settlement is yet small, but few families; yet he thinks it growing fast, and will soon form to a society," he said.

Chapter 3

December 1776: Riflemen, scouts leave Sunbury for the battlefields of New Jersey

Throughout 1776, the Pennsylvania frontier enjoyed the pastoral tranquility that Philip Vickers Fithian had described the previous year. The war continued, but its battles and skirmishes occurred far to the east of the Susquehanna settlements—at such distant places as Long Island, White Plains, and Fort Washington. In late 1776, news reached the Susquehanna Valley that the British and Hessians had routed the Continentals in and around New York City, forced them to cross the Hudson River, and pushed them southwest across New Jersey toward the Delaware River. Alarmed by these reports, many Susquehanna frontiersmen hurried east to reinforce Washington.

One of these men was Hawkins Boone, a surveyor whom Northumberland County records place on the West Branch before 1773. Boone had erected a mill along Muddy Run just above the stream's junction with the West Branch at some point before December 18, 1776. That was the day on which Boone, captain of a company of soldiers in the newly organized 12th Pennsylvania Regiment, boarded a boat in Sunbury, and, along with other men, "left Sunbury . . . for the battlefields of New Jersey," according to a regimental history in the Pennsylvania Archives. Most of the recruits were described as "riflemen and scouts," and many had been "recruited upon the West Branch."

The 12th took part in several skirmishes in New Jersey during 1777: at Bound Brook on April 12, Piscataway on May 10, and Short Hills on June 26. When Colonel Daniel Morgan's corps of riflemen was organized that summer, "a detachment from the 12th Pennsylvania, under the command of Captain Hawkins Boone, was placed in it," the history notes.

Although some early historians identified Boone as a cousin of Daniel Boone, an 18th-century frontiersman who achieved fame in Kentucky, genealogical data provided by The Boone Society doesn't show a link between Hawkins and Daniel. Born in Pennsylvania in 1734, Daniel Boone was the son of Squire Boone, who emigrated from England in 1713. Although Hawkins Boone was apparently born in Pennsylvania in 1745, his roots go back to 17th century Maryland. Hawkins' grandfather, William Boone, was born in St. Mary's County, in 1671, and his father, Abraham Boone, was born in Queen Anne's County prior to July 22, 1728. The Boone Society Inc. is a non-profit organization devoted to identifying and preserving Boone-related documents, artifacts, and historical sites.

Whatever his ancestry, Hawkins Boone and the other Pennsylvania riflemen found themselves headed up the Hudson River in mid-1777. That autumn, a major battle awaited them north of Albany at Saratoga, New York. As General Washington wrote to Major General Israel Putnam on August 16, "The people in the Northern Army seem so intimidated by the Indians that I have determined to send up Colonel Morgan's corps of riflemen who will fight them in their own way. They march from Trenton tomorrow morning."

"I expect much from them," said Alexander Hamilton, then an aide to Washington, in an August 18 letter to Robert Livingston in New York. "They are a picked corps, well used to rifles and to wood-fights, commanded by officers of distinguished bravery, and have been very serviceable in frequent skirmishes with the enemy."

Morgan and the riflemen soon distinguished themselves at the Battle of Saratoga, a two-part affair fought on September 19 and October 7, 1777. Morgan's sharpshooters contributed greatly to the American victory over the British and Hessian troops led by General John Burgoyne.

Chapter 4

May 1778: Indian raids terrorize the Susquehanna Valley

Iroquois war parties accompanied by British Loyalists repeatedly raided the upper Susquehanna Valley during early 1778. As these attacks began, West Branch homesteaders living north of Muncy Creek started to gather near a sharp bend in the river on property owned by Samuel Wallis and known as Muncy Farm. Wallis, a wealthy landowner, may have even let the settlers erect a stockade on his tract. Colonel Hunter, writing from Fort Augusta on May 26, reported, "they are all fled to Samuel Wallis's, where they intend to make a stand until the militia . . . marches up to their assistance."

Four days later, Hunter reported his county desperately needed more rifles, gun flints, and ammunition. "We are not quite out of ammunition, yet it's not when it's wanted that we should have to send for it," he said.

The previous week, an Indian raid on the Loyalsock settlements near present-day Williamsport had precipitated a panic. "It was really distressing to see the women and children from all quarters running to places the men had appointed to make a stand," Hunter said in a May 30 letter to George Bryan, who had become governor the previous week. Hunter noted that there hadn't been any new attacks for several days, but all along the West Branch, the settlers were "making little forts to leave their families in," he reported.

The refugees at Muncy Farm included three homesteaders from New Jersey—John and Judah Thomson, and their child, a small boy. The Thomsons had established a farm along Miller's Run in what has become Williamsport. At first, Thomson stayed with his wife and son at Wallis's, but on June 10 he returned to his farm, which was about a mile west of the Loyalsock, apparently to see how it had fared in his absence. Another man, Peter Shufelt, and a 16-year-old boy, William Wyckoff, accompanied him.

By June 10, Colonel Peter Hosterman, commander of the Northumberland County Militia's 3rd Battalion, had posted soldiers at Muncy Farm. On that date, Hosterman, Captain Reynolds, and a detachment of 13 troops left Wallis's and headed up the West Branch for the fort at Antes Mill, about 30 miles upriver. They were taking ammunition to the militia soldiers posted at the mill and higher up at Big Island.

The militia soldiers had traveled about five miles "and had just crossed the (Loyalsock) Creek (when) they heard a firing and yells" coming from up the creek," Hosterman said later. "They pushed on to the firing as fast as they could," but the Indians were gone "when they came to the place where they thought the firing was."

The soldiers then hurried through the forest and proceeded to the Thomson farm, which was "about a mile from the place they first heard the firing. . . ." Hosterman reported, "Just before they came to the house they heard two death halloos and one that they took to be a prisoner halloo." The colonel said that his soldiers "supposed from the yells that the Indians gave they were about 14 in number."

Fort Augusta occupied the east bank of the Susquehanna River just below the confluence of the river's West and North branches at Sunbury. Its guns controlled boat traffic on the river. The Northumberland County Historical Society erected this scale model on the site of the original fort.

The Indians had departed by the time the soldiers arrived. They had torched the barn, which "contained grain in the sheaf," but left the house untouched. Although they "saw several moccasin and shoe tracks" and "found Thomson's powder horn—with a bullet hole through it—near the house," the soldiers failed to find Thomson and his companions.

"This firing at Thomson's began between 2 and 3 o'clock and lasted about three-fourths of an hour," Hosterman said. "Our people had a very ugly swamp to cross through, which took them near a quarter of an hour." The delay kept them from reaching the Thompson farm in time to be of any help.

Later that afternoon, 16 west-bound travelers left Wallis's along the wagon road that followed the river. There were "six men, two women, and eight children . . . going with a wagon to Lycoming," a small village at the mouth of the Lycoming Creek where settlers had built a crude stockade. The village was about eight miles west of Muncy Farm.

When they neared the Loyalsock, a settler named John Harris warned them that he had heard shooting in the woods and that "to go forward was dangerous," but Peter Smith, who owned the wagon, "said that firing would not stop them." So the travelers, who included Smith's wife and six children, went on. The party also included William Snodgrass, a West Branch settler who in December 1776 was listed as a private in Captain Cookson Long's company in the Northumberland militia's Second Battalion.

After they left, Harris hurried to Wallis's and told the militia officers about his conversation with Smith. Captain Hepburn soon marched off with 14 men to find Smith. A war party found him first. Hidden behind trees along the road, the warriors attacked the wagon just before sundown. "When Smith with his wagon and party had got within three-quarters of a mile of Lycoming, the Indians fired at them," Colonel Hosterman reported later. "At the first fire, Snodgrass fell dead, being shot through the temple."

The warriors fired twice. Then they started to "shout and advanced running to the wagon . . . Our men . . . did not see them till they received the two fires." They rushed behind trees "and returned the fire. A little boy and a girl made off about this time. The Indians closed in very fast and endeavored to surround them." Four of the defenders "fled as fast as they could," but Michael Campbell, a militia soldier in Captain Reynold's company, stayed at the wagon, "fighting at close quarters with his rifle, and the Indian's gun was found broke to pieces." The men who ran off said that "before they were out of sight of the wagon, they saw the Indians attacking the women and children with their tomahawks."

David Chambers, another militiaman, said later that he thought there were about 20 members in the war party.

Captain Hepburn's detachment arrived from Muncy too late to be of help. They found two dead bodies on the ground, "but it being dark they could not distinguish who they were," Hosterman said. The captain and his men spent the night at Lycoming.

In the morning, the villagers and the soldiers went out to investigate. They found five dead bodies, all scalped. The sixth victim, William King's wife, was gravely injured but still alive. "Tomahawked and scalped, she was sitting up . . . but leaned on her husband when he came to her and expired immediately. She appeared sensible but could not speak," Hosterman said.

They also found the bodies of two children—a little girl and a boy.

Snodgrass had been "shot through the head, tomahawked and stabbed."

The valiant Campbell had been "shot in the back, tomahawked, stabbed, scalped and a knife left in him," Hosterman said. "They took . . . his rifle."

Later that day, soldiers from Muncy Farm went to the Thomson homestead and made an extensive search. They found the bodies of Thomson and his friend, Peter Shufelt, laying on the side of a field near some pines. "Thomson was shot through the left side and through the powder horn and scalped," Hosterman said. "Shufelt was shot through the left shoulder and scalped. They lay but a little distance apart." The Indians "were so near Thomson when they shot him that his jacket was burned." William Wyckoff, the teenager who had accompanied Thomson, had been wounded and taken away as a captive.

Chapter 5

July 1778: Continental troops arrive to defend the West Branch Valley

In July, a large force of Iroquois and Loyalists invaded the North Branch and killed more than 200 Americans defending the Wyoming Valley settlements in what became known as the Battle of Wyoming. In the days after the battle, hundreds of settlers fled from the Wyoming Valley. In turn, West Branch homesteaders fled from their homes in an event known as the Great Runaway.

Soon after these events, Continental soldiers came up the West Branch and spent seven weeks erecting Fort Muncy on Wallis's property during the late summer of 1778. Located about two miles north of the mouth of Muncy Creek, the post was built on a bluff and contained a covered passageway that led from the fort to a nearby spring.

As "colonel commanding on the Northern Frontiers of Pennsylvania," Lieutenant Colonel Thomas Hartley of the 11th Pennsylvania arrived at Fort Augusta with a detachment of 100 Continentals in late July. He had served in the American expedition to Canada in 1776, and as a brigade commander in the 1777 battles of Brandywine Creek, Germantown, and Paoli.

There were an additional 200 militia troops waiting for him at Sunbury. "Upon my arrival, I have taken the command," Hartley wrote.

The same month, Hawkins Boone and three other riflemen "were ordered home . . . to assist Colonel Hartley in protecting the West Branch Valley," according to the regimental history.

Hartley quickly saw the need to erect a strong fort at Wallis's. "On the 2nd of August, we were ordered by Colonel Hartley to build this fort," Captain Andrew Walker wrote months later. "We immediately began and finished by the 18th of September." Although the men completed the stockade wall, "we had built neither barrack, store or magazine" inside the stockade, the captain said.

When the exterior of Fort Muncy was complete in late September, Hartley used the new fort to stage a 15-day, 300-mile raid deep into hostile territory on the upper North Branch. On September 20, Hartley left an officer and 18 men to man the new post at Wallis's and started out on his overland expedition to Tioga. Boone went along.

Hartley's 200 soldiers followed the Sheshequin Path, which left the West Branch a short distance west of Fort Muncy and headed northeast, reaching the North Branch at the native village of Sheshequin (modern Ulster) some 70 miles away. At Sheshequin, Hartley swung north and marched upriver to Tioga (present-day Athens, Pennsylvania), an Iroquois town. Some 300 hostiles—"most of them Tories, dressed in green," Hartley reported—"had been at Tioga a few hours before we came." They were gone by the time Hartley's strike force arrived. "We burned Tioga . . . and all the settlements on this side," the colonel reported later.

The Indians retaliated on September 29 as Hartley's force descended the river, headed for Wilkes-Barre. They attacked a short distance below Wyalusing. Many of Hartley's men were marching along a well-used Indian trail called the Great Warriors Path

July 1778: Continental troops arrive to defend the West Branch Valley 29

Colonel Thomas Hartley built Fort Muncy along the West Branch between present-day Muncy and Williamsport in August 1778. Photo courtesy of the Muncy Historical Society.

that linked Tioga with the Wyoming Valley and, farther downriver, the Susquehanna confluence at Sunbury. Boone, Captain John Brady, and some others accompanied the marchers in canoes. At a critical point in the firefight, "Captains Boone and Brady . . . with a few brave fellows, landed from the canoes," and helped turn the fight against the natives. The Indians fled when "the war hoop was given by our people," Hartley said. "We advanced on the enemy on all sides, with great shouting and noise."

It was early October when the troops returned to Fort Muncy. "Bad weather coming on, we began our barracks, magazine, storehouse, etcetera," Captain Walker reported. "When this was finished, we were comfortably prepared against the winter." As an extra defense, the men surrounded the fort with a wall of logs that had sharply pointed ends. The logs were placed at an angle so that the wall leaned away from the fort. This created a barricade that enemy soldiers would need to climb before reaching the fort's vertical walls. An obstacle of this type was called an abatis.

The winter of 1778-79 proved to be severe, and this was especially hard on the fort. "In the spring I found the works much impaired," Walker explained in an April 17 letter. "I then set the garrison to repair the works and raised them eighteen inches. Then we put two rows more of abatises round the works. This is just now finished." The captain didn't explain how the height of the fort had been increased.

Addressed to John Hambright, a Northumberland County representative on the Pennsylvania Executive Council, the letter praised the performance of the soldiers, then noted that Pennsylvania hadn't ever paid them.

Throughout the time the soldiers were working on the fort, "one third of our men were constantly employed as guards to the inhabitants, and, I may affirm, in harvest the one half were employed the same way, nor can any man in the county say he ever asked a guard (when he had a just occasion) and was denied," the captain asserted.

During this time, "the troops were not supplied even with ration whiskey" and were "almost naked for want of blankets and clothes," Walker said. Despite this, "I have the satisfaction to inform you they done their duty cheerfully. I from time to time did promise them some compensation for their trouble and industry. The works are now finished, and, in my opinion, tenable against any number our savage enemy can bring against it."

Chapter 6

Hawkins Boone fortifies his mill on Muddy Run

By early 1779, Hawkins Boone had erected a log stockade at his mill just above the point where Muddy Run flowed into the West Branch. Dubbed Fort Boone, the mill and fort stood not quite three miles north of present-day Milton. Colonel Hunter had posted a small garrison there.

Boone had good reason to fortify his establishment. Gristmills and sawmills had become frequent targets of Indian raids. As frontier farmers had begun converting forests to fields, Boone and other millers had settled along fast-flowing streams and established small gristmills, often with milling machinery that they had imported from distant settlements. Mills were frequently constructed along or near old Indian trails, and frontier farmers used the trails to transport wheat, corn, rye, and other commodities to the mill for processing.

In the early 1770s, for instance, Jacob Vreeland had hauled milling equipment overland in wagons when he emigrated from New Jersey. Settling along the Warrior Run, a tributary of the West Branch, Vreeland soon had a gristmill operating on the stream. When Indians began raiding the Susquehanna settlements, Vreeland erected a log stockade around his homestead, which his neighbors, anglicizing his

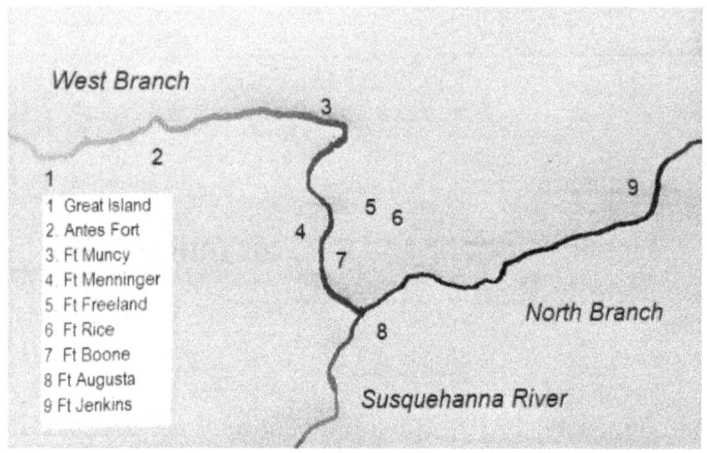

1. Great Island
2. Antes Fort
3. Ft Muncy
4. Ft Menninger
5. Ft Freeland
6. Ft Rice
7. Ft Boone
8. Ft Augusta
9. Ft Jenkins

surname, dubbed Fort Freeland. Fort Freeland stood about six miles northeast of Fort Boone.

Known as The Widow Smith, Catharine Smith established a complex of mills along the West Branch at the mouth of White Deer Creek three miles north of Boone's. By late 1775, she had a grist mill, sawmill, hemp mill, and a boring mill that cut rifling grooves inside gun barrels. In early 1778, a fort—known as Fort Menninger—was erected on the creek's north bank to the west of her mills.

Some 30 miles to the west, Henry Antes established a gristmill at the mouth of Antes Creek in the early 1770s. When Indians began raiding the region, Antes built a fort near the mill on a bluff overlooking the river. Elected captain of a militia company in 1776, Antes eventually became a colonel. His mill and fort stood on the West Branch opposite present-day Jersey Shore.

A Maryland miller named Bosley obtained land within the forks of Chillisquaque Creek at Washingtonville. He brought slaves with him and established a gristmill there before 1775. When the Indian raids began, Bosley erected a stockade at his mill, which

Hawkins Boone fortifies his mill on Muddy Run   33

This monument was erected on the site of Fort Freeland, which a force of Iroquois and Loyalists destroyed in July 1779, near present-day Turbotville. Looking on is Randy Watts, a descendant of James Watts, a setter who was killed at the beginning of the attack.

became known as Fort Bosley. Eventually, 20 militia soldiers were posted there.

1779 saw a spate of Indian attacks along both branches of the Susquehanna. In the spring, Widow Smith's mills and the nearby fort were evacuated when the Iroquois raided the West Branch Valley. Continental troops belonging to the 11th Pennsylvania responded to repel them.

The regiment also maintained a garrison at Fort Jenkins, a post that overlooked the North Branch about midway between the modern towns of Berwick and Bloomsburg. This fort played an important role in protecting commercial and military boat traffic up and down the river.

"Not a day but there is some of the enemy makes their appearances on our frontiers," Colonel Hunter reported to Governor Reed on April 27. "On Sunday last, there was a party of the savages attacked the inhabitants that lived near Fort Jenkins . . . but . . .

about 30 men turned out of the fort and rescued the prisoners. . . . Yesterday, there was another party of Indians, about 30 or 40, killed and took seven of our militia that was stationed at a little fort . . . called Fort Freeland. . . . The same day a party of 13 of the inhabitants that went to hunt their horses about four or five miles from Fort Muncy was fired upon by a large party of Indians. . . . Captain Walker of the Continental troops, who commands at that post, turned out with 34 men to the place he heard the firing, and found four men killed and scalped."

At Fort Jenkins, "the Indians collecting themselves in a body drove our men under cover of the fort, with the loss of three men killed and four badly wounded," Hunter said. Before the raiders left, "they burned several houses near the fort, killed cattle, and drove off a number of horses."

Command of the 11th Pennsylvania had passed to Lieutenant Colonel Adam Hubley of the 10th Pennsylvania following Hartley's resignation in February. A veteran of the 1777 battles of Brandywine and Germantown, Hubley had been posted in New Jersey. He arrived at Fort Augusta in mid-June.

On June 21, writing to Governor Reed, the colonel remarked, "At present, everything about this (region) seems quiet. The refugees here talk of returning again to their farms. I'm in hopes they will be able peaceably to enjoy them." Hubley added that Continental troops were stationed at Fort Augusta, Fort Jenkins, and Fort Muncy: "Duty is exceedingly hard, those places being posts of the greatest importance in this quarter, and require the strictest attention and alertness."

During the summer, General Sullivan's Continental regiments gathered at Wilkes-Barre as they prepared to invade the Iroquois country. Sullivan had expected Pennsylvania to provide troops for the campaign. When the state failed to comply by late

June, he ordered Hubley to withdraw the 11th Pennsylvania from the Northumberland County posts and to march them some 60 miles upriver to his encampment in the Wyoming Valley.

Colonel Hunter realized that Hubley's departure would open the way for new raids by hostile natives. He objected strenuously. In a June 26 report to Governor Reed, the militia commander said bluntly, "Colonel Hubley's regiment marches immediately, which leaves Fort Muncy and Fort Jenkins vacant at this critical time."

Hardly had Hubley's troops departed than the Iroquois raids resumed. "Immediately after the evacuation of Fort Muncy, the Indians began their cruel murders again," Hunter reported to Colonel Matthew Smith on July 23.

Written at Fort Augusta, Hunter's July 23 letter to Smith detailed attack after attack:

- On July 3, the hostiles "killed three men and took two prisoners at Lycoming."
- On July 8, "they burned the Widow Smith's mills and killed one man."
- On July 17, "they killed two men and took three prisoners" near Fort Brady at present-day Muncy. "The same day they burned Starrets Mills and all the principal houses in Muncy Township."
- On July 20, "they killed three men at Freeland's fort and took two prisoners."

With the Indians "sticking so close to this county after the Continental troops . . . marched to Wyoming, . . . the people . . . are really on the eve of deserting the county entirely," Hunter said.

Historical marker notes that Warrior Run Church Cemetery near Turbotville, Pa., contains the unmarked grave of Colonel Matthew Smith of the Lancaster County Militia.

As Hubley's Continentals headed upriver, Hunter assessed his strengths. "What few men Captain (Thomas) Kemplen had under his command was stationed at Bosley's mills on Chillisquaque," he wrote.

Many of the region's young men weren't available for militia service because they were employed as boatmen on the Susquehanna, shipping supplies upriver to Sullivan's staging area at Wyoming. Moving scores of flat-bottom boats up and down the Susquehanna required large numbers of workers. Consequently, "the county was quite drained of men by the boat service," Hunter complained. Meanwhile, "the few spirited men that remained had charge enough to guard the women and childer (children) at the different little posts they were assembled at."

Hunter added, "All the militia I could collect exclusive of what was at Fort Freeland and General Potter's was about 30, which I ordered to stay at Sunbury to guard the stores there."

The colonel struck a prophetic note: "Without some reinforcements, . . . it's not probable the little forts we have at Freeland's and Boone's can stand long." In a postscript, he added, "We are scarce of ammunition, especially lead. There is none."

By late July, Captain Kemplen and the garrison at Fort Bosley had shifted a dozen miles west to Fort Boone. That's where they were on the morning of July 28 when they suddenly heard gunfire coming from the direction of Fort Freeland, about six miles to the north along the old Shamokin Path. Boone and Kemplen quickly "marched off with 34 men to reinforce the fort at Freelands, but was *(sic)* met a little ways on this side by a number of the savages, who surrounded them immediately," Colonel Hunter reported six days later. Outnumbered, "our men behaved with great bravery for some little time, but . . . was almost cut to pieces. Our loss there was 15 killed and two wounded."

The colonel said the dead included "two very good men"—Hawkins Boone and Captain Samuel Dougherty.

By the time the men with Boone and Kemplen shot it out with the Indians, a large force of Loyalist rangers and Iroquois warriors had already captured, then burned Fort Freeland. The attackers suffered few casualties and took more than a score of prisoners—older boys and men. The captives were eventually taken to Fort Niagara as prisoners. The 50 women, children and elderly men captured at Fort Freeland were released and went down to Fort Augusta. Dr. Francis Alison Jr., a militia surgeon, was at Fort Augusta on the day after Fort Freeland fell.

The women told the surgeon they had seen "thirteen scalps . . . brought into the fort (Freeland) in a pocket handkerchief, amongst whom were Captain Boone('s) and Dougherty's."

"Boone's Fort is evacuated and Northumberland Town is already the frontier," the surgeon said.

Hunter was quick to inform Sullivan that Fort Freeland had fallen, but the general wasn't moved. "Your situation," the general told Hunter, " . . . must be unhappy. I feel for you, and could wish to assist you, but the good of the service will not admit of it." Suggesting that Hunter rely on the Pennsylvania state government for reinforcements, Sullivan advised, "Nothing can so effectually draw the Indians out of your country as carrying the war into theirs. Tomorrow morning, I shall march with the whole army for Tioga."

Writing to Governor Reed on August 4, Hunter reported the capture of Fort Freeland: "The enemy . . . has plundered and burned the country within 10 or 12 miles of Northumberland Town on the West Branch."

Chapter 7

November 1779: The German Regiment stationed at Susquehanna forts

With 4,000 troops, Sullivan's army vastly outnumbered the Iroquois. Statistics are scarce, but in 1763, there had only been 1,950 warriors in the entire Iroquois Confederacy. The Continentals overwhelmed the natives. There were few battles. As the soldiers advanced, the Indians withdrew toward Fort Niagara on Lake Ontario.

Sullivan marched to within 90 miles of Fort Niagara but returned to Pennsylvania in late September without attacking it. By the time the Continentals reached Tioga, they had destroyed 41 Iroquois towns along with the orchards, cornfields, and granaries belonging to the Indians.

As Sullivan had predicted, Indian raids had all but stopped in the Susquehanna Valley. By then, a war party had already destroyed Fort Muncy, following the departure of Colonel Hubley's Pennsylvanians.

During October, most of Sullivan's soldiers returned to the war's eastern theater in New Jersey and other seaboard states. As the campaign ended, Fort Augusta briefly served as a hospital for sick and wounded Continentals. By late October, most of these men were gone.

Late in the month, a Continental outfit known as the German Regiment was ordered to Fort Augusta.

Early in the war, the officers and rank-and-file soldiers for this regiment had been recruited from the Germans living in Pennsylvania and Maryland. Battle-tested in the years since then, they had seen combat at Trenton, Princeton, Brandywine, Germantown, and Monmouth before joining the Sullivan Expedition.

The German troops left Wyoming on October 29 and headed down the North Branch to Sunbury. They arrived at Fort Augusta with orders to strengthen the military presence in the upper Susquehanna Valley. Their commander was Lieutenant Colonel Ludwig Weltner, and he and Colonel Hunter soon sat down to determine the best way to distribute Weltner's troops.

The raids on the Freeland, Boone and Smith mills had underscored Colonel Hunter's need to defend the region's mills. Of the four places where Hunter thought troops should be posted, two were mills. He told Weltner that he wanted "a sergeant's guard at Bosley's Mills on Chillisquaque and another sergeant's guard at Titzell's mills in Buffalo Valley." These mills occupied strategic spots along the region's few roads.

Titzell's mills consisted of a gristmill and a sawmill along the Little Buffalo Creek on a 50-acre tract five miles northwest of present-day Lewisburg. A miller named Henry Titzell had established them during the winter of 1774-1775. When British and Indians threatened to invade the West Branch Valley in 1778, hundreds of families fled. Titzell had joined the exodus and never came back. Although this mill was never fortified, Hunter eventually assigned a small detachment to live at the mill and to patrol the Buffalo Valley.

Hunter also wanted to rebuild Fort Muncy on the West Branch. The British and Indians burned it during the summer, and Hunter felt a strong need to

Henry Titzell's gristmill in present-day Union County was never fortified, but a small detachment of Pennsylvania militiamen was stationed at the mill. Local residents have long referred to the site as Fort Titzell.

replace it. Indeed, he told Colonel Weltner that "the most effectual support and protection to the distressed Inhabitants was to rebuild Fort Muncy and garrison it with 100 men."

Hunter also wanted to station 25 men at Fort Jenkins, about 30 miles above Fort Augusta on the North Branch. Built in late 1777, the post consisted of a stockade that surrounded the house of a merchant named Jenkins. It sat on a high bank overlooking the river. Throughout the summer of 1779, it served as a frequent overnight stop for boatmen and soldiers shipping supplies up the river to Wyoming.

Hunter had anticipated that Colonel Weltner would bring 200 men with him but was both surprised and disappointed to see him arrive with a substantially smaller force. As Hunter complained in a November 27 letter, "I was informed the regiment consisted of 200 men, but instead of that number, there was but 120 effective men exclusive of officers." Of these, "we had but 60 men to order out to the frontiers, as the commanding officer is resolved to keep the one half with himself in Sunbury to relieve the others monthly."

Captain Frederick William Rice of the Continental Army's German Regiment built Fort Rice about 20 miles due north of Fort Augusta at Sunbury. This stone structure survives.

To their credit, the colonels did what they could with the men they had. Rather than rebuild Fort Muncy, they compromised and decided to construct a new post west of present-day Washingtonville at a place known as McClung's, apparently in the general vicinity of the ruins of Fort Freeland. Weltner sent a detachment there in early November, but reported that the men "found this place so void of shelter and so barren of timber that they were obliged to abandon it. . . . This detachment accordingly moved to a place called Montgomery's nearer to Bosley's Mill and equally well situated for the defense of the frontier."

Weltner's men constructed a stockade and then built a fieldstone barracks inside it. Captain Rice commanded the men stationed at this post and directed its construction during the winter of 1779-80.

It soon became known as Fort Rice. Indians had burned the Montgomery farm earlier in 1779.

The region seemed peaceful. Then a murder occurred along Muncy Creek in the West Branch Valley on November 5. "A certain James Clark was killed and scalped," Colonel Matthew Smith reported in a November 24 letter from Paxtang, near present-day Harrisburg. Smith said he had just returned from Northumberland County, where the killing took place in early November.

The manner of Clark's death tempted the authorities to suspect an Indian, but Smith and Hunter had their doubts.

"Various are the conjectures whether he was killed by the savages or some of our own people," Hunter said. He explained that "the reconnoitering party we had out" had found "no signs of any Indians or discoveries of any known enemy being on our borders at that time."

Colonel Smith expressed his view bluntly: "It is a matter of doubt whether it was done by Indians. It is my opinion it was not, as numbers of hunters have been out a great way up both branches and not the least sign or trace of Indians since General Sullivan and the army returned."

Before winter set in, Weltner and Hunter were able to staff the most strategic posts, but personnel levels were lower than Hunter had wanted. "There is but 40 men at Montgomery's Fort 12 miles on this side (of) Fort Muncy and 20 men at Fort Jenkins," Hunter reported to Governor Reed. In addition, Captain Kemplen and his company of 14 rangers were stationed about 17 miles from Sunbury at Fort Menninger on White Deer Creek, the West Branch tributary.

For his part, Weltner wrote in a December 13 report from Sunbury, "The detachments to Montgomery's and Jenkins have left me only men enough at Sunbury to mount a couple of sentries. I (cannot) erect any new posts without abandoning those already occupied, and the season of the year forbids such a measure."

As 1779 drew to a close, neither colonel reported any new Indian attacks. Welter's chief concern dealt with food. "Not only the posts, but even Sunbury is likely soon to be destitute of provisions," he said in a December 13 letter to the federal Board of War, an agency created by Congress to oversee the war effort. "Upon my arrival at Sunbury the commissary of purchases applied to me to write down to Colonel Cox and use my influence verbally . . . to have provisions brought up, particularly some salt . . . I did so but without effect. . . . The salt is only now arrived, and the cattle are miserably fallen away. Flour and liquors we are now at last informed are not to be had. I am sensible the purchases in this county are trifling and will not support us."

As winter came on at Sunbury, Hunter remained dubious that Sullivan had forced the Iroquois out of the war. True, Sullivan's soldiers had burned many towns, but they had killed few hostiles, and Hunter fretted about the possibility of future raids against his region. Heavy snow was falling at Fort Augusta as Hunter wrote to Governor Reed on November 29. "I hope . . . it will put a stop to the savages from making inroads on our frontiers till towards spring," he said.

Chapter 8

January 1780: Iroquois warriors shiver, starve, plot revenge

As they invaded the Iroquois homeland, General Sullivan's Continental soldiers sometimes entered a native town to find the people gone, but their food still cooking. On the evening of September 3, for instance, the soldiers "discovered a cornfield . . . and found the Indians had just then quit it, leaving corn roasting at the fires," wrote Lieutenant William Barton of General Maxwell's New Jersey Brigade. These natives had joined thousands of other Indians fleeing to Fort Niagara.

Colonel Daniel Brodhead, the commander at Fort Pitt, had led a smaller punitive expedition up the Allegheny River during August and September. Departing from their base at Pittsburgh, Brodhead's 600 soldiers went nearly 200 miles up the Allegheny and destroyed at least eight native towns and related farms. The cornfields had exceeded 500 acres.

By all accounts, the American offensives had forced a large number of pro-British natives to fall back on Fort Niagara for food. "On November 4, 1779, 3,329 Indians drew rations at Niagara," wrote historian Colin C. Calloway. "The majority—959 Senecas, 583 Cayugas, 435 Delawares, and 182 Chugnuts—were refugees from the Sullivan-Brodhead invasions." The refugees clustered around Niagara also included

Taken inside Fort Niagara along Lake Ontario in western New York, this photo looks across the mouth of the Niagara River to Canada.

smaller numbers of Mohawks, Tuscaroras, Oneidas, Nanticokes, Shawnees, and Mahicans, according to Calloway in his 1995 book, *The American Revolution in Indian Country.*

The Chugnuts had lived in a village along the Susquehanna River's North Branch near present-day Endicott, New York. The Continental soldiers burned it in August.

Calloway's statistics come from the correspondence and papers of Sir Frederick Haldimand, a British military officer who served as governor of Quebec during the Revolution and who oversaw activity at Fort Niagara. Haldimand's materials reside in the British Museum, London.

The winter of 1779-80 proved severe. In western Pennsylvania, "such a deep snow and such ice has not been known at this place in the memory of the eldest natives," Colonel Brodhead reported from Fort Pitt at Pittsburgh on February 11. "Deer and turkeys die by hundreds for want of food. The snow on the Allegheny and Laurel Hills is four feet deep.

In western New York, "the snow fell about five feet deep," recalled Mary Jemison, an adopted Seneca who survived the winter. The Senecas and other natives suffered greatly, "and some actually died of hunger and freezing," Jemison said.

Sullivan's soldiers had penetrated the Iroquois country during the harvest season. They not only burned all the towns and farms they encountered, but they also destroyed all the food the Indians had put away for the winter. At Little Beard's Town on the Genesee River, for instance, the Continentals "destroyed every article of the food kind that they could lay their hands on. A part of our corn they burnt and threw the remainder into the river," Mary Jemison said later. That winter, the natives congregated around Fort Niagara and turned to the British for provisions, but the fort lacked sufficient supplies to meet the demand. Heavy snowfalls frustrated native hunters. "Almost all the game upon which the Indians depended for subsistence perished," Mary Jemison recalled years later. ". . . When the snow melted in the spring, deer were found dead upon the ground in vast numbers. . . ."

As the Iroquois shivered and starved at Fort Niagara, hundreds of angry warriors resolved that when winter ended they would avenge Sullivan's invasion by raiding the American frontiers to their east. Indeed, some didn't wait for winter's end. Presumably wearing snowshoes, they headed east in early February, long before the snow had melted. They soon met a small party of eastern Iroquois bound for Fort Niagara. They had come to urge the Iroquois around the fort to make peace with the Americans. One of the four, a Mohawk chief known as Little Abraham, said the Continental Congress would offer peace provided that the Iroquois returned to their old territories and laid down their arms. The chief reported that before leaving eastern New York, he had obtained the support of an American general, Philip Schuyler,

Little Abraham's initiative failed. The warriors that he had met on his way to Niagara continued their journey and carried out their raids of revenge. Many other war parties soon followed. Throughout the year, warriors left Niagara in quest of revenge. "At least 60 Indian war parties left Niagara each year in 1780–1," Calloway wrote, again citing the Haldimand papers.

As Barbara Graymont wrote in *The Iroquois in the American Revolution:* "For the next eight months, the Iroquois warriors would ravage the white settlements with a steady and furious assault. Between February 11 and July, a total of 495 Indians and whites . . . went out on service. After July 1, about 400 at a time would be ranging the frontiers."

War parties out of Fort Niagara posed the greatest danger for the frontier settlements in central and eastern Pennsylvania, but Indians supplied by the British at Fort Detroit also menaced western Pennsylvania. The posts at Niagara and Detroit were nearly 250 miles apart. Fort Niagara was 250 miles north of Fort Pitt. That made it slightly closer than Fort Detroit, which was 280 miles northwest of Fort Pitt.

Military leaders in western Pennsylvania saw the danger of their situation. "It is reported the savages are drove to Niagara and Detroit, and there supported by the British," Colonel Alexander Lochrey of the Westmoreland County Militia said in a January 9 letter written at Hannastown, the Westmoreland County seat 30 miles east of Pittsburgh. "If this be so, we may expect their visits early next spring, and, it is generally thought in such bodies that we cannot withstand them," Lochrey told Governor Reed.

At Fort Pitt, "I am really apprehensive of a visit from Niagara," Colonel Brodhead advised the governor in a

February 11 letter. Brodhead said he had learned from an informant "who has frequently been at Detroit" that "the new fort erected there is very strong." It had "walls 15 feet thick and very high, with a wide, deep ditch surrounding it."

The informant had reported that "the garrison consists of 450 regulars and that the enemy have 1,800 men besides a great number of Indians at Niagara," Brodhead said.

By February 27, Brodhead had received "intelligence from Sandusky" on Lake Erie's

Joseph Reed, a Philadelphia lawyer, served as president of Pennsylvania's Supreme Executive Council for several years during the American Revolution. His responsibilities made him the state's de facto governor, and he was frequently addressed as Governor Reed.

southwestern shore that warned of a possible assault against Fort Pitt later in the season. The colonel's source had reported "that at least 2,000 of the enemy Indians which were driven into Niagara were encamped on the plains near that place," which was nearly 300 miles from Fort Niagara.

The British were possibly planning "an expedition against this garrison so soon as the Allegheny should be filled with a sufficient quantity of water to favor the attempt." In other words, the British and Indian allies would descend the river, swollen by the snowmelt as well as spring rains, in canoes and boats. "As the enemy's approach by water would be exceeding rapid," Brodhead had decided to take defensive measures to strengthen the fort. One of these involved posting a few men in a house that occupied high ground within 40 yards of one of the bastions and commanded the cannon in two bastions. The structure, "being barricaded, would greatly contribute to the defense of this post," the colonel told Richard Peters of the Board of War in a February 27 letter.

Indian raids resumed well before winter ended. On March 12, gunshots shattered the peace of a maple grove where settlers were collecting sap and making maple syrup along a tributary of the Ohio River northwest of Pittsburgh. "The savages have already begun their hostilities," Colonel Brodhead wrote to Joseph Reed on March 18. "Last Sunday morning at a sugar camp upon Raccoon Creek, five men were killed and three lads and three girls taken prisoners."

People were quick to suspect "that the Delawares have struck this blow, and it is probable enough, but it is possible it may have been done by other Indians," Brodhead said. "If the Delawares are set against us with their numerous alliances, they will greatly distress the frontier as my force is quite too small to repel their invasions."

The colonel advised the governor that he had written "to the commander-in-chief for a reinforcement from the main army, but I fear it will not be in his power to detach any of the troops." He added that he had asked the Board of War "to forward some ordnance and military stores without which our parts cannot well be defended nor offensive operations carried on."

Chapter 9

March 29: The capture of Lieutenant Moses Van Campen

As the winter of 1779–80 yielded to spring, many Susquehanna Valley homesteaders believed that General Sullivan had "completely vanquished" the Iroquois. "Now it was perfectly safe for the farmer to return to his employments and, as soon as the spring should open, commence the labor of cultivating his soil." Or so Lieutenant Moses Van Campen of the Northumberland County Militia told his grandson some six decades afterward.

Author Charles Miner came to a similar conclusion while researching his 1845 *History of Wyoming*. "Being confident that Sullivan had left in the whole Indian country nothing for them to subsist upon," many Wyoming Valley settlers believed that the Iroquois "were necessarily within the British lines at Niagara, beyond striking distance; and the settlers resumed their farming at Kingston, Hanover, and Plymouth, the latter seven miles distant from the Wilkes-Barre fort. A few adventured further. The main settlements had block-houses built, in case of attack, wherein to seek shelter and make defense."

All too soon, these people learned how mistaken they were. One such person was Lieutenant Van Campen. An experienced Indian fighter who had participated in the Sullivan Campaign, he knew that the Continental Army had laid waste to many native towns, destroyed the cornfields and orchards, and burned the granaries where the Indians had stored their harvest.

Born in New Jersey in 1757, Van Campen was the oldest of 10 children. He grew up in the Delaware River Valley and moved with his parents to present-day Columbia County in the 1770s. He helped his family establish a farm along Fishing Creek, which flows into the North Branch at Bloomsburg.

When the Revolution began, the young man joined the Pennsylvania militia and in 1777 served a three-month tour with Colonel John Kelly at the western-most settlements along the Susquehanna River's West Branch. Van Campen had attained the rank of lieutenant by age 20.

As Samuel Hazard reported in an 1833 edition of *Hazard's Register of Pennsylvania*, "In the spring of 1777 Van Campen took the command a small detachment of . . . men, and built a small fort on the waters of Fishing Creek." Dubbed Fort Wheeler, this post was a log stockade, situated several miles above the mouth of the creek.

As the Sullivan Expedition geared up in the spring of 1779, Van Campen spent several months buying provisions for the army from Susquehanna Valley farmers and merchants and then arranged to ship the supplies up the North Branch to Sullivan's staging area in the Wyoming Valley. He went along as a volunteer rifleman when the army invaded the Iroquois country.

By early 1780, Van Campen had returned to the North Branch, convalescing at Fort Wheeler from a fever. His hiatus from soldiering let him spend time with his family. With peace now restored across the frontier, the scout intended to help his father and brother rebuild the family farmhouse that a war party had burned two years earlier.

Despite the deep snow, Van Campen accompanied his father, brother, uncle, cousin and a man named Peter Pence as they left Fort Wheeler in late March, headed for the Van Campen homestead. His father and uncle each had farms, "about half a mile apart and four miles distant from the fort," Van Campen said. "Not anticipating danger, they had only two rifles, one with each company, and in other respects, were wholly unprepared for an attack from their foes."

On March 29, 10 Iroquois warriors caught Van Campen's uncle by surprise at his farm, killed him and his son, and captured Peter Pence. "Taking possession of the rifle," the Indians then made their way to the neighboring farm. Attacking swiftly, they killed and scalped Van Campen's father and brother, and captured Van Campen, who became the war party's third prisoner. The Indians already had Pence and a boy named Jonah Rogers.

The Indians led their captives into the hills, following Fishing Creek. They camped in the woods that night. In the morning, they resumed walking. At the head of Hunlock Creek, which joins the North Branch below Nanticoke, they encountered a man, woman, and child making sugar in a maple grove. This wasn't surprising. In late winter, many frontier families went into the woods to collect sap from the sugar maples.

The Indians hid and forced Van Campen to call out to them. The man was identified later as Abraham Pike, who had settled in the Wyoming Valley. "In a moment Pike came running up, and when he was just at hand, the savages rushed out upon him, with their tomahawks, and brandished one over his head," Van Campen said. "The poor fellow immediately dropped on his knees and begged for quarters."

The Iroquois terrorized Pike and his family. One warrior "took the little child by the heels and swung it around, with the intention of dashing out its brains against a tree," Van Campen said. "The infant screamed, and the poor mother, with a frantic shriek, flew to its relief, catching hold of the warrior's arm." At this point, one of the leaders interceded. He gave the child back to its mother and told her that she should leave. He even pointed the way back to the settlements, but before he let her go, "taking out his paint box, (he) painted her," Van Campen said.

Shaken but safe, the woman was still wearing the Indian's paint when she reached Fort Wyoming at Wilkes-Barre. As Lieutenant John Jenkins wrote in his journal for March 30: "Mrs. Pike came in this day, and informed that she and her husband were in the woods making sugar, and were surrounded by a party of . . . Indians, who had several prisoners with them, and two horses. They took her husband and carried him off with them, and painted her and sent her in. They killed the horses before they left the cabin where she was. One of the prisoners told her that the Indians had killed three or four men at Fishing Creek."

As Mrs. Pike headed for Wyoming, the war party resumed its northward trek. As Van Campen reported in his 1842 autobiography, the "route over the mountain was very difficult, and in many places the snow was deep. They came to the North Branch . . . at Little Tunkhannock Creek where the Indians had moored their canoes after descending the river. When they had crossed over to the east side, the canoes were propelled into the middle of the stream and set adrift."

The reason for letting the canoes drift downriver was obvious. They wouldn't be available for use by soldiers who might be tracking the war party.

The warriors led their prisoners along a trail that followed the river, and Van Campen realized the Indians intended to take them to Fort Niagara. He realized that the Iroquois would be especially cruel to any white prisoners brought into their region that spring. He decided that he and the two other prisoners needed to attempt an escape even though the Indians outnumbered them.

As his grandson wrote six decades later, Van Campen told the other captives that since "they were the first prisoners . . . taken in after the destruction of the Indian villages and corn by Sullivan the summer before, they would in all probability be tied to the stake and subjected to a cruel and lingering death." The captives agreed to attempt an escape. After all, "if they failed, it would only be death, and they might as well die one way as another," Van Campen said.

As an 1833 edition of *Hazard's Register of Pennsylvania* reported:

"On the night of the second of April, about 12 o'clock, the prisoners concluded that all the Indians were sound in sleep. Van Campen had previously procured a knife. They rose, cut themselves loose, and immediately removed all the (Indians') arms." The warriors didn't stir, and the captives quickly tomahawked some and shot others. The Indians who survived fled into the forest without any clothing or weapons.

Van Campen and his comrades hurriedly scalped the dead Indians and collected the scalps the warriors had taken from settlers. Then they gathered up as many guns and other goods as they could carry, and hurried toward the river, where they built a raft and set sail for Wyoming.

Lieutenant Jenkins wrote about their arrival at Wilkes-Barre in his journal for April 4: "Pike and two men from Fishing Creek . . . made their escape by

Tourists walk through the gate at Fort Niagara. In 1780, Iroquois war parties took prisoners captured in Pennsylvania to the fort. Lieutenant Moses Van Campen escaped as his captors traveled toward Iroquois settlements near the fort.

rising on their guard of 10 Indians—killed three—and the rest took to the woods naked, and left the prisoners with 12 guns and about 30 blankets, etc. These the prisoners got safe to the fort."

Abraham Pike and the boy Jonah Rogers remained at Wilkes-Barre, and Van Campen and Pence obtained a canoe and came downriver. When they reached Fort Jenkins below present-day Berwick, they learned that everyone there had feared that Van Campen and the other prisoners had been killed.

After that, "I went to Sunbury. . . . I was received with joy, my scalps were exhibited (and) the cannons (at Fort Augusta) were fired," Van Campen told his grandson John N. Hubbard. In 1842, Hubbard published a book about the old soldier's experiences. It was titled, *Sketches of Border Adventures in the Life and Times of Moses Van Campen.*

Chapter 10

Ferocious firefight erupts along the upper Delaware

On April 21, a ferocious firefight erupted between native raiders and frontiersmen on a Pennsylvania farm along the upper Delaware River between the present-day communities of Milford and Dingman's Ferry. The skirmish, which began about two miles south of Milford, ended with several men dead on both sides. As they inspected the site of the fighting after the war party left, the settlers made a significant discovery: The enemy dead included a white man, "an officer appearing by his dress," said John Van Campen, a Lower Smithfield farmer who had served as a justice of the peace before the war. John Van Campen and Moses Van Campen were different people.

The dead officer had been keeping a journal, which the settlers found in a pocket. Journal entries began on March 1 and continued through April 16. "As appears by his journal there is (sic) 390 marched from (Fort) Niagara, divided into different parties," Van Campen said in an April 24 letter to Governor Reed. The letter didn't list the officer's name.

Van Campen described the episode in detail. A Pennsylvania farmer, James McCarty, had moved his family across the Delaware River to New Jersey but continued to keep livestock on his Pennsylvania farm. Van Campen said the McCarty farm, "where the attack began, is about two miles below Well's Ferry." According to Alfred Mathews, in *History of Wayne, Pike, and Monroe Counties, Pennsylvania*, the ferry was in Milford.

On April 20, McCarty's sons crossed the river and went to the farm to feed the cattle. Alarmed to see signs of Indians, they returned to New Jersey at once and notified officers of a nearby militia company. "They sent immediately for some of their best men and crossed the river that night," Van Campen said. Around sunrise the next morning, the militia "discovered the Indians nigh the barn and began the attack. The number of the enemy is supposed to be about 14. The major received no damage with his party. The Indians retreated to the woods."

At this point, reinforcements showed up in the form of five Pennsylvania militiamen—Captain John Van Etten, who lived about a mile south of the McCarty farm, arrived along with three of his sons and a son-in-law. At least one Indian was wounded, and the militia troops "pursued the Indians by the blood, and (after) about two miles came up with them." The frontiersmen renewed the attack, and the Indians "ran to the edge of a thick wood." The firefight ended with casualties on both sides. The Indians fled, and the Americans later found the bodies of an Indian and the Loyalist officer.

The May 3, 1780 edition of the New Jersey Gazette reported that the defenders had three dead. In addition to the two dead men, "the Indians left behind them six blankets, two watch coats, several packs and a quantity of provisions."

Chapter 11

April 25: Raiders torch Gilbert's mills, take 15 captives

Well before sunrise on Tuesday, April 25, 1780, a farmer named Samuel Dodson sent his 14-year-old daughter Abigail with a sack of grist to a mill that Benjamin Gilbert operated on Mahoning Creek, a tributary of the Lehigh River 25 miles north of Allentown. As the Pennsylvania Gazette reported eight days later, the farmer wanted his daughter "to fetch some meal."

The Dodson farm was about a mile from the mill, which Gilbert had constructed after moving to the Mahoning from Philadelphia in 1775. The mill was located several miles west of the present-day Carbon County community of Lehighton.

Soon after Abigail's arrival, an Iroquois war party attacked the mill complex. Quakers, the Gilberts didn't resist, and the Indians quickly seized control. Several warriors guarded the Gilberts while "the rest of the captors employed themselves in plundering the house, and packing up such goods as they chose to carry off, until they had got together a sufficient loading for three horses, which they took," the Gilberts said later. They also distributed some of the plunder among the captives and directed them to carry it.

Twelve warriors conducted the raid, and they took the elderly miller and 12 members of his extended

Mahoning Creek powered the mills that Benjamin Gilbert operated four miles west of present-day Lehighton. In April 1780, an Iroquois war party captured Gilbert and 12 members of his extended family and took them to Fort Niagara. Two other Pennsylvanians were also captured.

family away as prisoners. At 69, Gilbert was the oldest captive. Gilbert's 9-month-old step-grandchild was the youngest. Abigail Dodson became the 14th captive, and Andrew Harrigar, a 26-year-old laborer employed by Benjamin Gilbert, became the 15th.

When a militia patrol came by two days later, "we found Mr. Benjamin Gilbert's house and gristmill and sawmill totally consumed with fire," Lieutenant Nicholas Kern told Colonel Samuel Rea, commander of the Northampton County Militia. Since the war party had a two-day head-start, "we were not able to overtake them, but we could have followed their tracks to Susquehanna," Kern said.

In a trek that took a full month, the warriors forced the Gilberts to walk more than 300 miles to Fort Niagara. Surviving family members said later that the Indians took them north through the Wyoming Valley, then up through New York's Finger Lakes before turning west and heading toward Lake Ontario and the British fort.

Located a short distance from the Mahoning Creek, the monument marks the location of the Benjamin Gilbert mill complex and commemorates the Gilbert family's experience. Its inscription says: "In memory of the Benjamin Gilbert family and others who were taken captive by the Indians April 25, 1780. Benjamin Gilbert his wife Elizabeth, Joseph, Jesse, Sarah, Rebecca, Abner, Elizabeth and Benjamin Gilbert, Thomas and Benjamin Peart, Elizabeth Peart and her 9-month-old baby, Andrew Harrigar and Abigail Dodson. Erected by Lehighton Chamber of Commerce, Lehighton, Pa. Dedicated September 9, 1928."

In time, British soldiers at Niagara transported nearly all the captives to Montreal on the St. Lawrence River. The miller died before he reached Montreal, but the others left Montreal and returned to Pennsylvania two years later. They subsequently told the story of their ordeal to William Walton, a relative of Elizabeth Gilbert, who published a book about it in 1784.

On the morning of the raid, while most of the Indians plundered the Gilbert residence, several warriors went to a house about half a mile away and returned to the mill with three more prisoners—a man and woman and their baby, all members of the extended Gilbert family.

The raiders were soon ready to depart. As the warriors led their prisoners away, two Indians set fire to the mills and other buildings. As the Gilberts walked up a nearby hill, "they could observe the flames and the falling in of the roofs," Walton said.

With the captives in tow, the war party hurried north. The travelers halted for an hour after crossing Broad Mountain, and at some point struck the Nescopeck Path, an Indian trail that coursed northwest to the Susquehanna River's North Branch. They stopped for the night on a ridge that Walton called "Mahoniah Mountain."

The prisoners quickly learned that life on the trail would be quite harsh. The first night, for instance, they watched as the warriors made a special structure to secure them for the night. They used their tomahawks to chop down a sapling "as large as a man's thigh," then cut deep notches in the log. Placing the sapling flat on the ground with the notches on top, they forced the prisoners to lay on their backs with their legs in the notches. The warriors placed a pole over the top of their legs, and then fastened the pole and the sapling together, "effectually confining the prisoners on their backs."

For good measure, the Indians placed a strap around the neck of each captive and fastened the strap to a tree. "In this manner, the night passed," Walton said. "Their beds were hemlock branches strewed on the ground, and blankets for a covering."

On Friday, April 28. They "were all painted according to the custom among the Indians, some of them with red and black, some all red, and some with black only," Walton wrote. The survivors later told Walton that those painted black had been marked for death. The writer didn't say which captives had been blackened.

April 25: Raiders torch Gilbert's mills, take 15 captives   63

The war party took the Gilberts up this hill as they started walking to Fort Niagara. Before they left, the Indians torched the buildings, and family members said later that they could see the fire from the hillside.

On Saturday, April 29, the Indians awoke to find that their horses had strayed during the night. It took several hours of searching to find them. When they resumed their march, they "kept the course of the river, walking along its side with difficulty." In the afternoon, they came to a place where four runaway black slaves awaited them. A week earlier, as the warriors headed south to raid the settlements, they had encountered these slaves traveling north. When the Indians challenged them, the runaways said they were loyal to King George and "were on their way to Niagara."

The Indians invited the four to join the group. As they traveled, the runaway slaves began to torment the Gilberts, "frequently whipping them for . . . sport, and treating them with more severity than even the Indians themselves," Walton said. The brothers who led the war party, Captains Rowland and John Montour, didn't prevent this.

Black slaves weren't uncommon in Pennsylvania during this time. Indeed, the 1886 *History of Wayne, Pike, and Monroe Counties, Pennsylvania* listed 26 slaves—men, women, and children—living north of the Blue Mountain in what was Northampton County in 1780. Although Walton didn't give the names of the runaways accompanying the war party, the 1886 survey reported male slaves had such names as Dick, James, Pompey, Abraham, and Thomas.

On the 10th day—Thursday, May 4—the travelers came to a fork in the trail. Several warriors took four prisoners along the trail that headed west. The other 11 captives all went with the main group, which headed north. At dusk, a prisoner with the main group asked about the captives who had been separated. An Indian replied, "These were killed and scalped, and you may expect the same fate tonight."

The statement terrified Andrew Harrigar, the hired man. Harrigar, "as soon as it was dark, took a kettle with pretense of bringing some water, and made his escape under favor of the night," Walton wrote. The Indians searched all night, but Harrigar eluded them. In the morning, the remaining captives were "treated with great severity" and accused of helping the man escape. Walton reported that although Harrigar "endured many hardships in the woods," he eventually made his way back to the Pennsylvania settlements.

Some of the warriors regularly hunted for deer as the war party herded the captives along. After nearly two weeks on the trail, the travelers reached Iroquois towns near Watkins Glen, New York, near the southern end of Seneca Lake. Eight months earlier, the Iroquois had abandoned these towns as Sullivan's army approached. The Indian hunters continued to provide venison. As the prisoners passed the farms that

Sullivan's soldiers had burned, they supplemented the venison by scouring the fields for "turnips and potatoes, which had remained in the ground, unnoticed by the army."

The farther north they traveled, the scarcer food became. At the northern end of Seneca Lake the previous September, the Continentals had found the town of Canadasaga with about 60 houses surrounded by apple and peach orchards. Nearby fields had contained so much corn, beans and squash that "our soldiers lived very bountifully on vegetables, etcetera, while here," reported Lieutenant John Jenkins, a Wyoming Valley soldier who served Sullivan as a guide. Before they moved on, the Continentals burned the village, chopped down the orchards, and destroyed whatever food they didn't eat.

Seven months later the warriors and captives couldn't find any food in Canadasaga. By noon on Sunday, May 14, the war party reached the Seneca town, which was near present-day Geneva, New York, not quite 40 miles north of Watkins Glen. The warriors had sent a messenger ahead with a request for provisions, and spent much of the day at Canadasaga, waiting for food to arrive. Eventually, two white men came with a small supply of hominy and maple sugar.

Despite their hunger, the captives had a pleasant surprise: in the town were Sarah Gilbert and the young Benjamin Gilbert, "two of the four who had been separated from them . . . and taken along the western path," Walton said. "This meeting afforded them great satisfaction." The two other prisoners —Joseph Gilbert and Thomas Peart—eventually arrived in the Iroquois refugee settlements near Fort Niagara.

Hunger continued to torment the travelers. Four days later, on Thursday, May 18, a warrior mounted one of the horses and rode off. He returned on foot several hours later "with a large piece of meat, ordering the captives to boil it. This command they cheerfully performed, anxiously watching the kettle, fresh meat being a rarity which they had not eat(en) for a long time," Walton reported. When the meat was sufficiently boiled, each warrior took a piece and ate sparingly. "The prisoners," Walton said, "made their repast without bread or salt, and (ate) with a good relish what they supposed to be fresh beef, but afterwards understood . . . was horse-flesh."

Four weeks on the trail had left the prisoners raggedy, dirty and gaunt. Also, the warriors had forced them to cut their hair quite short. On Tuesday, May 23, as they approached the Seneca town where Captain Rowland Montour lived, they saw that men, women, and children had gathered to meet them and that they carried rocks and clubs. Two of the women—Walton doesn't identify them—arrived on horseback, but the Indians frightened the horses, and the women fell off and "were much bruised," Walton said.

The villagers began beating the prisoners as they entered the town. "Elizabeth, the mother, . . . received several violent blows, so that she was almost disabled," Walton reported.

The prisoners were virtually defenseless against blows to the head. With their hair cut short, "the blood trickled from their heads in a stream," Walton said.

The beatings ceased only when a chief "put a stop to any further cruelty," Walton said. After that, the villagers helped the captives tend to their wounds.

Benjamin and Elizabeth Gilbert were taken to Captain Montour's house, where the women treated them kindly and gave them something to eat. "Two officers from Niagara Fort, Captains Dace and Powell, came to see the prisoners . . . Benjamin Gilbert informed these officers that he was apprehensive they were in great danger of being murdered upon which they promised him they would send a boat the next day to bring them to Niagara," Walton wrote.

In time, the British soldiers arranged for the Gilberts to sail across Lake Ontario and down the St. Lawrence to Montreal. Benjamin Gilbert died during the voyage. The surviving family members lived in Montreal and weren't permitted to return to Pennsylvania for nearly a year after the British loss at Yorktown, Virginia, in October 1781.

Even so, Abigail Dodson, the 14-year-old neighbor who had come to the mill for meal on the morning of the attack, remained an Indian captive. At some point, as other members of the Gilbert party were being released, Abigail "inadvertently informed the Indians she was not of the Gilbert family," Walton said. After that, "all attempts for her liberty were fruitless."

According to the Buffalo, New York, Historical Society, in 1784, after Great Britain and the United States had formally ended the war, Abigail Dodson's "friends found her and took her home to Pennsylvania."

Chapter 12

William Maclay's appeal: 'Help us if you can'

In late March, Iroquois war parties began raiding the Susquehanna Valley settlements above Fort Augusta.

"The savages have made their appearance on our frontiers in an hostile manner," Colonel Hunter reported to Governor Reed in Philadelphia on April 2.

"The day before yesterday they took seven or eight prisoners about two miles above Fort Jenkins, and two days before that carried off several people from about Wyoming. This has struck such terror . . . that all the settlers above this will be in the towns of Sunbury and Northumberland before two days," Hunter said, writing from Fort Augusta.

Information coming in from the country north of the Susquehanna's confluence at Sunbury convinced William Maclay that a force of Indians had overwintered in the hills at the head of Fishing and Muncy creeks. "They were with us to the very beginning of the deep snow last year. They are with us now before that snow is quite gone," Maclay reported in a letter, also dated April 2, to the governor.

Maclay explained that in late 1779 "many of our hunters . . . went out . . . into that country, which is a fine one for hunting." They became "so alarmed with constant reports of guns, which they could not believe to be white men's, that they returned suddenly."

Maclay and Hunter saw an obvious need to determine the truth of the situation. That meant sending scouts deep into the region. but "we are not strong enough to spare men to examine this country and dislodge them," Maclay told Governor Reed, ". . . Help us if you can."

William Maclay

Hunter noted that the spring planting season was an especially critical time for the Susquehanna's farmers. "If they miss getting spring crops put in the ground for the support of their families, they have nothing that can induce them to stay," the colonel said.

Colonel Weltner had stationed troops of the German Regiment at strategic posts: Fort Augusta at Sunbury, Fort Montgomery on the Chillisquaque, and Fort Jenkins on the North Branch. Already spread thin, these soldiers couldn't provide additional relief. In addition, so many members of the Northumberland County militia were farmers preoccupied with spring planting, that "calling out the militia of this county" wasn't an option. "Our case is really deplorable, and without some speedy assistance being ordered here, I am afraid the county will break up entirely," Hunter warned.

He implored Reed to have the state's Executive Council "order some of the militia from our neighboring counties to act in conjunction with the few Continental troops that's here. . . . Without something like this . . . to encourage the people, I dread the consequences that may ensue."

Hunter pointed out that Northumberland County had taken a severe drubbing in recent years. Only 12 months earlier, "we had a pretty good fort garrisoned at Muncy of Continental troops (and) Brady's Fort and Freeland's with our own inhabitants, but now we have but about 40 or 50 at Montgomery's, and 30 at Fort Jenkins."

When a war party attacked the settlements just north of Fort Jenkins on March 31, there were "not above 30 Indians and Tories in the party." They had taken a number of captives. Hunter noted that "a pretty deep snow had fallen the night before" and the raiders and their prisoners would have been easy to track. Even so, the commander "was not able to spare men enough out of the garrison to pursue the enemy . . ."

"I have seen the time within this three years past that we could turn out some hundred of good woodsmen, but now the case is altered, as our county is quite drained of our best men," Hunter said.

Some of the information that Hunter, Maclay, and Weltner had recently obtained came from an unlikely source: members of an Iroquois war party. Never thinking that their prisoners might escape, the warriors who attacked the Fishing Creek settlements had bragged about British and Indian activity to Moses Van Campen, Peter Pence, and the other captives. Within days after their escape, Van Campen and Pence traveled to Sunbury and shared the intelligence with the authorities at Fort Augusta. Pence gave details of his captivity in a deposition, which Colonel Weltner forwarded to the Board of War.

In turn, William Maclay quickly relayed highlights of this intelligence to Pennsylvania officials in Philadelphia. The frontiersmen "are just come in," Maclay wrote from Sunbury on April 9. ". . . They had the following information:

- "That 100 Indians left Niagara last fall.

- "That they received as much clothing as they wanted, each man four blankets. When they came about Tioga, they found fat cattle which they killed and built themselves houses. They gave the prisoners some of the beef which was very fat.

- "That these 100 Indians all set off to war when they did. (... We know only of three parties having been down on this county, all of whom by the best accounts, amount to about 40.)

- "That they expected Colonel (Joseph) Brant with 150 warriors every day.

- "That as soon as the leaves were green, 550 Indians would strike at different places between Schenectady (N.Y.) and Fort Pitt.

- "That the British at Niagara paid them 50 shillings for a scalp and five pounds for a prisoner.

- "That three (Iroquois) towns were left untouched by General Sullivan, one of them a very large one."

Maclay emphasized that the Indian raids would continue as long as the British could subsidize them. "While the English continue to supply the Indians at Niagara, pay them and support them as at present, peace with the Indians (in my opinion) is unattainable," he contended. "We ought to have Niagara, cost what it will."

Maclay was interrupted as he wrote. "Colonel Hunter this moment calls on me," he said. "A fourth party of Indians struck last night at 9 o'clock at his plantation on the West Branch of Susquehanna about 15 miles from this place. A man and child were killed, and a woman taken. We do not know the strength of this party."

"The Inhabitants have been flying this week past," Maclay said. He predicted that news of this raid would prompt many more settlers to leave: "I believe there will not be one family in Northumberland Town" by morning.

"You may easily guess that I am much hurried and far from being easy in mind, as I have my family amidst this confusion," Maclay said.

Colonel Weltner also received a report about this raid. "I have this moment received an express from the West Branch about 12 miles from this town that the Indians have killed and scalped one man and two children, took one woman prisoner, but she happily made her escape from them in the night," he said, writing from Northumberland, also on April 9.

The colonel had other news as well. Captain Anthony Selin, a Continental officer stationed at Wyoming, had sent him a letter reporting that Indian raiders had captured three Wyoming Valley settlers, but the prisoners had escaped. In the process, they had "killed two and wounded three of the Indians and brought in six rifles, one sword, and two tomahawks. They say upon their way up the river, they fell in upon two parties of Indians, one party (of) 25 and the other (of) eight coming down to fall on the West Branch."

Weltner reported that he had stationed members of the German Regiment at three outposts: Fort Jenkins, Fort Montgomery, and Bosley's Mills. "It is out of my power to scatter my men any more, as I have scarcely as many men in town as will man two pieces of artillery," he said.

Deteriorating conditions in the upper Susquehanna Valley warranted both additional troops and new shipments of supplies, especially food. "Without . . . a reinforcement sent to man the West Branch, I do really think the inhabitants will not be able to stand their ground," Weltner said. He added that unless his regiment soon received "a sufficient quantity of provisions, . . . I will be obliged to evacuate the post myself." Other critical supplies—especially ammunition and gun flints—were also running low, "these commodities being so very scarce."

Maclay's and Weltner's respective letters crossed with the governor's April 7 letter to Hunter. Reed said that the council wanted Hunter to "encourage the young men of the country to go in small parties and harass the enemy." To entice them, the council would pay cash bounties—$1,500 "for every male prisoner whether white or Indian," provided "the former is acting with the latter." There was a second inducement—"$1,000 for every Indian scalp. The proof must be left to your own discretion." The state wasn't offering bounties for the scalps of white people.

Hunter's reply, written on April 17, shows that the prospect of cash bounties for prisoners and scalps had an immediate effect: Susquehanna inhabitants were already "raising parties of volunteers to go in quest of Indians." As an extra incentive, the colonel was even "assuring them of rations and ammunition (during) the time they are out."

The Indian raids had continued. "Last Saturday (April 15) a party of 20 Indians struck at Peter Swartz's plantation about 12 miles from here on the West Branch," Hunter said. "They killed one man and wounded three." The wounded had come down to Fort Augusta, and Dr. Alison, the fort's surgeon, was caring for them.

The attack occurred at a time when three different groups of settlers were out on scouts. The scouts responded to the alarm, as did militia soldiers "stationed about two miles above where the Indians struck."

"A party formed as quick as possible and pursued the enemy," Hunter said. "Three or four that was on horseback riding smartly up came in sight of the enemy, which occasioned them to drop their packs and turn up the mountain. Our party pursued them all day, but could not come up with them."

William Maclay, a Northumberland County official, stored ammunition and other military supplies in the first floor of his stone house along the Susquehanna River at Sunbury. The second story was added during a 19th century renovation. MaclayHouse

According to local lore, Revolutionary War soldiers stationed at William Maclay's house in Sunbury inscribed their names in its exterior stone walls as they guarded military supplies stored in the dwelling. A name visible in this photo: ISAIH CASAE.

Chapter 13

Pennsylvania offers a reward for scalps of Indians

As Europeans colonized the Eastern Seaboard during the 1600s, they learned that native warriors often cut off—and kept as trophies—part of the scalp and hair of people that they had killed or wounded in warfare. This practice came to be known as scalping, and Europeans whose settlements were subject to Indian raids dreaded it. To be sure, the practice of scalping remained prevalent throughout the 18th century, during the American Revolution.

British military officers offered bounties on the scalps that their Indian allies brought back from the Pennsylvania frontier. Pennsylvania authorities eventually followed the British example. As letters written by Governor Reed make clear, the state began paying cash bounties for the scalps of hostile Indians in the spring of 1780.

James Thacher, a medical doctor who served as a surgeon in the Continental Army throughout the war, graphically described how native warriors scalped their enemies: "With a knife, they make a circular cut from the forehead, quite round, just above the ears, then taking hold of the skin with their teeth, they tear off the whole hairy scalp in an instant, with wonderful dexterity. This they carefully dry and preserve as a trophy, showing the number of their

Farmer carries musket while plowing.

victims, and they have a method of painting on the dried scalp different figures and colors to designate the sex and age of the victim, and also the manner and circumstances of the murder."

Governor Reed, in letters written during April and May 1780, informed militia and military leaders across the state that Pennsylvania would pay a reward for prisoners—Tories as well as enemy Indians—but that a bounty on scalps would be offered only on those taken from the heads of Indians.

In an April 11 letter, for instance, Reed directed Colonel Jacob Stroud at Fort Penn (present-day Stroudsburg) "to encourage the young men to hire out in small parties to endeavor to strike the enemy near home." The state had authorized payment of "$1,500 dollars for every Indian or Tory prisoner taken in arms against us, and $1,000 dollars for every Indian scalp," he explained.

On April 29, Reed notified Colonel Brodhead at Fort Pitt that "after many consultations and much deliberation, we have concluded to offer a reward for scalps and hope it will serve as an inducement to the young fellows . . . and others to turn out against the Indians."

In early May, Reed advised Colonel Samuel Rea of the Northampton County Militia of the new practice. Offering rewards for scalps and prisoners was intended to "encourage the young men of the county, and even of (neighboring) New Jersey, to turn out in small parties, endeavor to fall in with them on their marches, and even follow them to their towns," the governor said.

In Westmoreland County, Colonel Lochrey raised the issue of scalp bounties when he wrote to Reed on June 1 and requested the state to provide the county with an additional "500 or 600 weight of powder . . . and the same quantity of lead." The colonel explained that since his county was continually on a war footing, its defenders consumed immense amounts of gun powder. "Every man on the frontiers (is) obliged to carry their arms, even at the plough," Lochrey said. He added, "I hope the reward offered will answer a good end, as a number of people seem determined to exert themselves that way, for which reason the ammunition now applied for will be the more wanted."

Only Colonel Brodhead expressed any reservations about the new policy. He noted that not all Indians were hostiles. On the contrary, Delaware warriors "act with our scouts, and seem very desirous of discovering the enemy's parties," the colonel said. As for paying bounties for scalps, Brodhead told Reed in a May 18 letter, "I wish it may have the desired effect, but I apprehend that it will be construed into a license to take off the scalps of some of our friendly Delawares, and produce a general Indian war."

Chapter 14

War parties employ hit-and-run tactics in raiding settlements

War parties frequently used hit-and-run tactics with success. A mid-May raid on the grist mill that French Jacob Grozong operated on Rapid Run in Buffalo Valley serves as an example. The stream is a tributary of Buffalo Creek. The mill, located about 10 miles west of present-day Lewisburg, stood along a trail that led to a pass in the mountains forming the valley's northern side. The mill was about a mile east of the pass.

On May 16, hostile Indians ventured out of the gap, attacked the mill and killed four militia soldiers, and then hurried back to the safety of the mountains. "The neighboring inhabitants, on hearing the firing, briskly turned out, and pursued the enemy very brave, but was (*sic*) not able to overtake them," Colonel Matthew Smith reported. The neighbors showed up so quickly that "the enemy got only one of the scalps," Smith added.

Writing to Governor Reed from Northumberland on May 18, Smith apologized for the poor quality of his report. He wrote hurriedly because "General (James) Potter . . . waits on horseback, whilst I write this imperfect, distressed account."

Other attacks soon followed. "An Indian prisoner was taken about 10 days ago by one of the inhabitants

Erected in 1922, this marker commemorates a May 1780 attack on American soldiers at French Jacob's mill in western Union County.

about 10 miles up the North Branch and conducted to Sunbury jail," Colonel Weltner reported on June 20. "About the same time Mr. Lewis was killed in his own house, upon the road leading from Sunbury to Reading, being about seven miles from town."

A third incident involved Robert and Jane Curry who had settled along Mahoning Creek above present-day Danville. They were riding along the river when "Curry was shot off his horse about seven miles up the North Branch," Weltner said. He died, and Mrs. Curry was captured, but managed to escape, the "night being very rainy, . . . and came in (to Fort Augusta) the next morning. There was but two Indians she informs me, that they had used her very kind."

Despite these episodes, enemy activity appeared to be waning. As the weeks passed, it seemed to Weltner that there were fewer hostiles "on our frontiers at present." He sent out scouts accompanied by volunteers to reconnoiter "all the country for 40 miles up from the North to the West Branch." They had "made but little discoveries," the colonel said. "One officer and five volunteers went up the waters of the West Branch better than 100 miles. They discovered nothing but old encampments and old Indian tracks."

Writing to the governor, Colonel Weltner said that "I often reconnoiter my outposts, and shall go tomorrow again to see what discoveries I can make. Five or six gentlemen in this town and two of my officers are commonly my escorts as volunteers."

Colonel Hunter's June 27 letter to the governor indicated that the settlers' quest for scalp bounties had begun at a time when the enemy raids were slowing down. The colonel reported that several parties had gone into the woods "to get scalps or prisoners agreeable to the proclamation but . . . returned without success." These men had discovered Indian tracks "but could not make out which way they were bound." Meanwhile, no murders had been committed since the June 12 killing on the Reading road.

If bounty hunters brought in few scalps, at least one Indian prisoner was delivered to Fort Augusta. Hunter had him committed to the jail "where he remained till last Friday, (when) Colonel Mathew Smith took him down to Lancaster," Hunter told Reed. He added, "We had him examined here by an interpreter . . . He says he is of the Tuscarora tribe but talks the Mohawk tongue well."

The Indian had surrendered to a farm family living along the North Branch about 10 miles above Sunbury. On the same day as the Reading Road murder, Thomas Bowyers and members of his family were working in a cornfield near their farmhouse when "an Indian man came to the field" in a non-threatening

French Jacob Grozong built a small gristmill along Rapid Run, a tributary of Buffalo Creek about 10 miles west of present-day Lewisburg. A war party attacked it in May 1780.

way, Hunter reported. The Indian "clubbed his gun and stepped up to Bowyers to shake hands with him."

After this happened, "Bowyers' daughter desired the Indian to go to the house and there they would give him bread and milk The Indian readily complied and went to the house carrying his own gun all the time, but never attempted to do them the least injury." At the house, a son "took and tied the Indian and brought him to me," Hunter said.

The Indian told Hunter that "he was not with the party that had done the murder that morning," and that he "did not intend doing any harm to the white people, but wanted to come and deliver himself up."

The man who brought the Indian to Fort Augusta became more troublesome than the Indian. "Bowyers has demanded certificate from me to entitle him to the reward offered for prisoners agreeable to the proclamation," the colonel said. "I told him I could not with any propriety give him that." Instead, Hunter said he would refer Bowyers to the Executive Council and urged him to relate "the manner he took him."

Although June and July turned out to be somewhat peaceful months along the Susquehanna, Indian raiders remained active across other parts of the Pennsylvania frontier. In mid-July, for example, they killed 12 militia troops at a Bedford County outpost. As Colonel John Piper told Governor Reed in an August 4 letter, the dead included Captain Philips, "an experienced, good woodsman (who) had engaged a company of rangers for the space of two months." Phillips had been "surprised at his post on Sunday the 16th (of) July," along with eleven of his company."

Piper said he learned of the attack the next day. "I marched with only 10 men directly to the place, where we found the house burnt to ashes, with sundry Indian tomahawks that had been lost in the action." When they didn't find any bodies, Piper's men followed Indian tracks through the woods. "Within about one-half mile we found 10 of Captain Philips' company with their hands tied and murdered in the most cruel manner. The attack occurred "in a place called Woodcock Valley and not one of the party escaped," according to Colonel Abraham Smith of the Cumberland County militia.

Chapter 15

'I do not find that they ever stir a foot out of their posts'

Since its arrival at Fort Augusta in late 1779, the German Regiment had hardly endeared itself to Colonel Hunter of the Northumberland County Militia. To begin with, the regiment's commanding officer, Lieutenant Colonel Ludwig Weltner of the Continental Army, had brought only 120 rank-and-file troops, not the 200 that Hunter needed to strengthen the garrisons of outposts defending the county's remote settlements.

Months later, Hunter remained displeased. "The German Regiment that's stationed here is no ways adequate to grant us the necessary relief," he advised Governor Reed on April 2.

Hunter reported that on March 31, a party of about 30 Tories and Indians raided a North Branch settlement two miles north of Fort Jenkins, where Weltner had posted a garrison of 30 men. The hostiles had taken seven or eight prisoners. Because "a pretty deep snow had fallen the night before," Hunter believed that the raiders could have been "easily tracked." But Fort Jenkins "was not able to spare men enough . . . to pursue the enemy," Hunter said.

The regiment's critics included William Maclay, who had little good to say about it. "The German Regiment are posted at four different places, but I do not find that they ever stir a foot out of their posts without some other support," Maclay remarked in an April 9 letter to the Executive Council.

He added: "I cannot help uttering a wish that what troops we have might be all Pennsylvanians. There is a certain love of country that really has weight. This is a strange divided quarter. Whig, Tory, Yankee, Pennamite, (Pennsylvania) Dutch, Irish and English influence are strangely blended."

Colonel Weltner himself had engendered controversy, and complaints about him that originated in the Susquehanna Valley eventually reached Philadelphia. Without listing specifics, Governor Reed advised the regimental commander in an April 4 letter that "some misunderstanding has happened between the inhabitants of the county and yourself." He proceeded to admonish Weltner: "You must be sensible of the very great difference of treatment which is necessary in this country from that of Europe, and that it has a tendency to alienate the affection of the people from the troops." Reed added, "We hope as this is the first instance, so it will be the last of any complaint on this subject. We must particularly caution you against showing any resentment against the person complaining."

To be certain, Colonel Weltner had weathered his share of difficulties at Fort Augusta. Ever since the regiment had arrived, supplies had been difficult to secure. On May 6, writing from Northumberland, Weltner had advised the Board of War: "Am exceeding sorry to inform you that if I do not get a speedy supply of provisions, there being but six days' on hand, am afraid I shall be obliged to quit my post." He explained that without success he had communicated his need to downriver suppliers at Carlisle and Lancaster.

Within weeks of his arrival at Sunbury in late 1779, Weltner found himself the target of criticism. In an obvious reference to nearby Northumberland, the colonel said, "There is a rival town over the river which is not without its factious citizens." In a December 13 letter addressed to the Board of War, Weltner reported he suspected "that great part of the complaints . . . have originated with . . . a discontented commissary, who, 'tis said, is likely to be discharged and would throw all into confusion rather than be unemployed."

In the months since then, Weltner had come to dislike the Susquehanna Valley. Writing to General Washington on May 16, the colonel remarked, "I am sorry to be separated from your Excellency's army and to be stationed in such a wilderness, but for the good of the service am always content." In a June 20 letter to Governor Reed, Weltner expressed a personal complaint: "This place has not afforded a drop of good liquor since the beginning of March . . . This makes a commanding officer look little at the post where he is kept so poor."

As 1780 progressed, Hunter continued to press the governor for more troops. His April 2 letter, for example, asked Reed to "order some of the militia from our neighboring counties, to act in conjunction with the few Continental troops that's here."

The governor promptly rejected Hunter's request. "Anxious as we are to do you all the service we can, we have observed with concern that our measures for your relief have been dreadfully expensive to the state with little advantage to you," he said. The state government had significant troubles of its own. "Our situation is so critical and difficult that your own exertions must now be depended on. . . . With the assistance of the German Regiment, which is

Teamsters guarded by American soldiers moved military supplies over rough mountain roads such as this section of Forbes Road north of Cowan Gap between the south-central Pennsylvania villages of Fort Loudon and Burnt Cabins.

considered no inconsiderable support, we trust your difficulties will grow less," Reed wrote on April 7.

In his May 16 letter to Washington, Weltner noted that Indians continued to raid the upper Susquehanna if only infrequently. "About a month ago the enemy attacked this county in four different places, but had little success," he reported. The letter also gave additional details about the raid on French Jacob's mill in the Buffalo Valley: "And yesterday seven savages attacked 10 of our militia on an outpost, killed four the first fire, and the remaining six wounded two of the savages and made them make a precipitate retreat."

Within weeks, General Washington reassigned Weltner's regiment. By mid-summer, Washington decided that it had become "necessary for me to call the German Battalion from Sunbury to join this army," and that he needed to do so quickly.

Writing to Governor Reed from Peeks Kill, New York, on August 1, Washington noted that Congress had asked Pennsylvania "for men to fill her battalions" in the Continental Army. When Pennsylvania failed to meet its obligation, Washington decided to send the German Regiment elsewhere. "Had the requisition . . . been even nearly complied with, . . . I should have foregone the advantages which would have been derived from the service of this corps and continued it at its present station. But this not having been the case, I am compelled to avail myself of its aid," Washington said.

Unpopular as the German Regiment had become, news of Washington's decision caused consternation at Fort Augusta. Ineffective as the German troops might be, they were nonetheless better than no troops. Withdrawing the regiment—"weak as it is," in Colonel Matthew Smith's phrase—increased the county's vulnerability to attack. Northumberland officials sent a petition to the state's Executive Council in which they decried Washington's decision and declared that it put the county in a "defenseless situation." It asserted that with the German Regiment gone, the inhabitants "are not any longer able to support themselves against the inroads of the savages"

The petition, Smith said in a cover letter, "would have been signed by a much larger number, but the Indians making a stroke on Tuesday last at two different places, . . . none but delegates could possibly attend" the meeting at which the petition was adopted. "The people seem more discouraged than I ever saw them, and, indeed, are somewhat exasperated," said Smith, the county prothonotary.

With the Germans about to leave, Colonel Hunter became desperate for soldiers to replace them. Other counties came to his relief. "I have sent one company . . . to the frontiers of Northumberland County and the other to the frontiers of Bedford, which was in a very distressed situation," said Colonel Abraham Smith of the Cumberland County militia.

Colonel Frederick Watts of the Cumberland County militia said on September 16 that he had intended to send troops to Northumberland County, but "to our mortification when the men were ready to march, there was no ammunition." When he went to Carlisle and requested ammunition at the Continental Army's storage depot, Watts said that he "could get none from them without an order from the Board of War." He added that officers at the storehouse told him "that there was not a bit of lead in their possession."

Watts' remarks touched on an issue that had proved troublesome for military commanders across Pennsylvania throughout 1780. As early as February 27, writing from Pittsburgh, Colonel Brodhead reported that "the great depth of snow upon the Allegheny and Laurel Hills has prevented our getting every kind of stores, nor do I expect to get any now until the latter end of April." Although Brodhead didn't explicitly mention munitions, in a March 18 letter, he advised Governor Reed that he had recently asked "the Board of War to forward some ordnance and military stores without which our parts cannot well be defended nor offensive operations carried on."

On April 11, Reed informed Colonel Stroud of the Northampton County militia that a shipment of "200 pounds of powder, 800 lead, and 500 flints" was en route to the county. "We must recommend to you great care in keeping as well as economy in using the ammunition as it is grown a very scarce and difficult article to be procured," he said.

On June 1, Colonel Alexander Lochrey sent Reed a request for "500 or 600 weight of powder, or what Your Excellency may judge necessary, and the same quantity of lead, . . . and a quantity of flints will likewise be wanted" for use by the Westmoreland County militia.

Lochrey acknowledged that "Your Excellency may perhaps think there is too large a quantity of ammunition expended in this county, but . . . there is scarce any such thing to be purchased here."

When Indian raids resumed in the spring Lochrey had requested more ammunition. "I am sorry to inform your Excellency that I received but six pounds, and was informed . . . that a large quantity of it was damaged in the carriage over the mountains so that at this time I think we have not 20 pounds of good powder in the county of public property."

Colonel Hunter weighed in on June 27, stating bluntly, "We are scarce of ammunition in this county." He added, "That you made mention of to me in your letter of the 24th of April last has never come to hand so that I am a little apprehensive it has been miscarried."

Reed's retort was equally blunt: "The supply of ammunition sent you last April was very considerable, and as it is by no means in such plenty or so cheap as that we can afford these miscarriages."

The governor disclosed that in June 1779, Colonel Matthew Smith had received a shipment of "511 pounds of powder and 1,000 flints, which we are informed were not forwarded immediately, and are now supposed to be in Paxtang (present-day Harrisburg)."

Reed's tone was sharp: "We think this and the parcel sent last April should be inquired after and would prove a very competent supply at present."

Not surprisingly, Colonel Smith responded swiftly. The munitions had been shipped to Paxtang in June 1779, a time when Indian attacks forced many settlers to evacuate Colonel Hunter's region. "You will see by the order of council it was for the use of Lancaster and Cumberland Counties in case Northumberland broke up," Smith told Reed.

For good measure, Smith contended that the ammunition that Reed said had been "sent in April last has not come to hand . . . and (I) am apprehensive it did not come from Philadelphia." Smith added that he had been in Philadelphia in late April and had been unsuccessful in obtaining munitions for Fort Augusta. "Captain Hambright mentioned he had an order from council for ammunition, but at that time could not get a wagon to carry it to Estherton," a village just north of present-day Harrisburg where the Continental Army had established a supply depot. Smith added that at Hunter's request, "I called on Colonel Cox who informed me no ammunition had arrived this summer for Northumberland County but a few boxes of cartridges, and they were immediately forwarded to Colonel Weltner for the use of his regiment." Cox was an assistant quartermaster.

As the year progressed, officers of the county militias continued to press the state government for ammunition and other supplies. On August 6, for instance, Colonel John Piper provided Reed with a list of supplies needed in Bedford County: "500 weight of powder and lead . . . 1,000 gun flints, one dozen falling axes, six camp kettles (and a) ream (of) writing paper." Piper explained that "we are much distressed for want of the above particulars" and that "your compliance will be a means of encouraging what remains of the county to stand this season . . ."

In neighboring Cumberland County the next day—August 7—Colonel Abraham Smith sent a similar letter to the governor. "This county is now very scarce of ammunition, and I have not been able to find any trusty hand and wagon to send for any," Smith said. "But I expect one before long when I flatter myself that (the Executive) Council will supply us with a sufficient quantity of powder, lead, and flints."

Smith asserted that supplies of arms and ammunition had run so low that if all the militia troops ordered to turn out actually reported for duty, "we will not be able to arm them." He added, ". . . We have already furnished the volunteers out of what state arms was here. . . . We have yet a few muskets, but they all want bayonets."

Governor Reed attempted to satisfy these and similar requests, but the state government and Continental Army moved with agonizing slowness. As Colonel John Mitchell, a deputy quartermaster general, explained on August 11, "I have three ammunition wagons . . . I have wrote *(sic)* to Lancaster, Lebanon and Reading to send down all the covered wagons they have and, if any repairs are wanted, to get it done Immediately. . . . I have as yet received no answer but will send again this day to the several places above mentioned. I have now wrote to Colonel Moore to request he would endeavor to send in 10 open wagons with the utmost dispatch. I cannot place an entire confidence in receiving them, but believe he will do all in his power."

The governor suggested that Mitchell arrange to borrow wagons so that munitions shipments could be expedited. Even so, he appeared pessimistic. "I perceive I shall be much embarrassed with respect to the ammunition . . . wagons," he said.

Chapter 16

Mid-summer 1780: The German Regiment marches away

When the German Regiment marched off to West Point, New York, Colonel Hunter's top priority became replacing the Continentals with militia troops to garrison Fort Rice, which stood along a road linking Muncy and Fort Augusta at Sunbury; Fort Jenkins, along the North Branch about 30 miles above Fort Augusta; and Fort Swartz, a stockade on the West Branch farm of Peter Swartz about 12 miles above Northumberland.

Hunter also saw the need to have militiamen patrol the region regularly. He placed 20 men at each of the three forts, then assigned another 20 to patrol duty. "This was the only method I could think of encouraging the people as we were left to our own exertions," the colonel told Governor Reed.

The Indians and British soon moved to exploit the weakness created by Weltner's withdrawal. On September 6, "we were alarmed by a large party of the enemy making their appearance in our county," Hunter said.

According to Brigadier General James Potter, "a few men that was out from Fort Rice" discovered the hostiles and hurried back to the fort, "which discovery prevented the fort from being surprised." The militia troops managed to alert Colonel Hunter "of a large party of savages and Tories coming against Fort Rice."

As Hunter later reported to Reed, "the enemy attacked the fort about sundown and fired very smartly. The garrison returned the fire with spirit, which made them withdraw a little off, and in the night, they began to set fire to a number of houses and stacks of grain, which they consumed."

According to General Potter, the Fort Rice garrison had one man killed, and one man taken prisoner. Neither Potter nor Hunter listed casualties suffered by the Tories and Indians.

Hunter promptly ordered the militia to turn out. He also ordered the evacuation of Fort Jenkins "as I did not look upon it to be tenable."

The news of a sizeable enemy force moving across the West Branch Valley terrified the inhabitants, and "it was not easy to collect a party equal to fight the savages," Hunter said. Even so, 100 men responded, and he placed them "under the command of Colonel John Kelly who marched to the relief of the garrison, and arrived there the next day." The soldiers at Fort Rice told Kelly that they had been attacked by an enemy force of 250 to 300. Kelly realized that he was outnumbered and didn't pursue the invaders.

When Hunter learned that Lieutenant Colonel James Purdy of Cumberland County's 7th Battalion "was marching to the frontiers . . . with the militia," he sent an express rider to Purdy with word of the pending crisis north of Sunbury. "He came as quick as possible to our assistance with 110 of the militia, and about 80 volunteers, which was no small reinforcement to us," Hunter told Reed.

On September 10, General Potter, one of the top officers in the Pennsylvania Militia, had nearly arrived at his house in Penn's Valley, then part of Northumberland County, when he learned of the attack on

The September 1780 skirmish along the Little Nescopeck has become known as "the Sugarloaf Massacre" because it took place near a cone-shaped hill that reminded settlers of a loaf of sugar.

Fort Rice. He hurried the 50 miles from present-day Old Fort to Fort Augusta. "I set off that night," arrived at Sunbury, and assumed command of the force that Colonel Hunter had organized, Potter said later.

When Potter reached Sunbury, "I found by the spies that had been sent out that the enemy were not so numerous as at first was apprehended." Instead of 250, there were only about 100. According to Colonel Hunter, the immediate danger had subsided and a more realistic estimate of the hostile force had been determined. "The enemy did not exceed 150, and . . . they had withdrawn from the inhabitants to some remote place," Hunter said.

With a much smaller force to confront, General Potter decided that he had more troops than he needed and sent the volunteers, but not the militia, back to Cumberland County. "As soon as we could get provisions, which was the next morning, I marched the remainder, consisting of 170 men, up the West Branch to Fort Swartz," Potter said.

Mid-summer 1780: The German Regiment marches away 95

This monument commemorates the September 11, 1780 skirmish along the Little Nescopeck Creek in which Seneca warriors and Loyalists surprised a force of Pennsylvania militia and volunteers, killing 13 and capturing three.

It was September 12, and Potter "went to Colonel Kelly who lay at the mouth of White Deer Creek with 80 men. Our accounts of the enemy's route seemed uncertain. At that time we concluded to join the next morning and to proceed along the Muncy Hill towards Huntingtown (Huntington)."

Before Potter arrived at White Deer, Kelly had sent three spies up the West Branch to find the hostiles. When the spies failed to return at the appointed time, Colonel Kelly and his officers told Potter that "they were convinced that they were either killed or taken prisoners."

On September 13, the two columns moved up the river, "Colonel Kelley to march up that side of the branch his men were on, and I would go up the other side," Potter said. When the men got to Muncy, Kelly's "spies returned and assured us that the enemy had not gone up the branch," Potter reported.

At this point, the combined force swung east and followed the southern slope of Muncy Hill toward Fishing and Huntington creeks, north-south streams that drain the hilly terrain between Wilkes-Barre and Muncy. The Huntington flows into Fishing Creek about 11 miles before it joins the North Branch at present-day Bloomsburg. The soldiers were headed toward the settlements along these creeks when an express rider arrived with news that a war party had been spotted "in the neighborhood of Middle Creek," Potter wrote. "The next morning (September 14) I sent Colonels Kelly and Purdy back with 150 men."

Neither Potter nor Hunter provided details of enemy activity, if any, along the Middle Creek settlements. An east-west stream in present-day Snyder County is known as Middle Creek.

After Purdy and Kelly left, Potter continued east with a smaller force of about 110 men, "and that day came to the (place) where the enemy had lodged on their way coming down and returning the next day," after attacking Fort Rice. "We followed their tracks nearly opposite to Wyoming and found they were so far gone that it was in vain for us to go any further after them," Potter said. "We return(ed) without seeing one of the enemy."

Colonel Hunter reported afterward that Potter had found the road taken by the Tories and Indians "and followed on about 50 miles up Fishing Creek . . . but finding they had got too far ahead," Potter returned to Fort Augusta on September 17.

After Potter returned to Sunbury, "we all concluded the enemy had gone off, but on the 18th there was a small party made their appearance on the West Branch," Hunter said. The raiders attacked farmers who were planting late-season varieties about 14 miles above Sunbury. "They killed one man and wounded another, and killed the horses they had in the plow," Hunter said. He concluded that rather than remain in a large body, "they have scattered into small parties to harass the inhabitants, which I am afraid will prevent the people from getting crops put in the ground this fall."

In urging Governor Reed to send miltia troops to Fort Augusta, General Potter remarked, "the enemy burned and destroyed every thing in their power, and on their way going they . . . burnt the fort and buildings at Fort Jenkins, which had been evacuated a few days before on the enemy's appearing at Fort Rice."

In a postscript, Potter added, "I am informed . . . that a large body of the enemy crossed the Muncy Hill . . . and went up the Muncy Creek." This information prompted Potter to reassess the numbers of Indians and Tories that had come into the region. "It is likely that the number that was down amounted to near 300 men," he said. The general added that as they departed, "they carried off a large number of cattle and horses with them."

General Potter and Colonel Hunter were unaware that a week earlier a war party had attacked a militia force 50 miles east of Sunbury. In early September, the leaders of the Northampton County Militia at Easton had sent a party of 41 men, part militia soldiers and part volunteers, to the county's northern region along the North Branch. This happened after "small parties of the enemy" made repeated raids on the county's remote settlements. Among other things, the Northampton men were to determine "why a number of families on the enemy's borders remain on their farms without molestation . . ."

Commanded by Lieutenant John Moyer. the men left on September 8 and traveled by way of Fort Allen on the Lehigh River. Three days later, they encountered a force of Loyalists and Indians along the Little Nescopeck Creek, several miles northwest of present-day Hazleton. The militiamen "were attacked on the 11th at the Nescopeck by a party of white men and Indians who had the advantage of first fire on our men, which obliged them to retreat," Colonel Samuel Rea reported in a September 17 letter to the governor. "The enemy's loss we cannot ascertain, but the wounded and missing of ours, amount to 23," Rea said.

More detailed information came in over the next several days, and on September 20 Lieutenant Colonel Stephen Balliet, commander of Northampton's 1st Battalion, sent another report to Reed. Lieutenant Moyer's men had learned that "a number of disaffected persons lived near the Susquehanna at a place called the Scotch Valley, who have been suspected to hold up a correspondence with the Indians and the Tories in the country," Balliet said.

According to Balliet, "They sat out on the 8th . . . for that place to see whether they might be able to find out anything of that nature, but were attacked on the 10th at noon about eight miles from that settlement by a large body of Indians and Tories . . . One had red hair."

Some survivors estimated the size of the attacking force at 40, although others put the estimate at

In September 1780, the Northampton County Militia sent a detachment of 41 men on a scout toward the Susquehanna River's North Branch. They encountered a war party of Seneca Indians and Loyalists along the Little Nescopeck Creek at present-day Conyngham northwest of Hazleton. The Pennsylvanians suffered 13 dead and three captured.

"twice that number," the colonel said. "Twenty-two out of 41 have since come in, several of whom are wounded. It is also reported that Lieutenant John Moyer had been made prisoner and made his escape from them."

Moyer managed to escape, then made his way to Fort Wyoming at Wilkes-Barre. As Lieutenant John Jenkins wrote in his journal for September 14: "Lieutenant Myers from Fort Allen came into the fort and said he had made his escape from the Indians the night before, and that he had been taken in the Scotch Valley, and that he had 33 men with him, which he commanded. He was surrounded by the Indians, and 13 of his men killed, and three taken. This day we heard that Fort Jenkins and Hervey's Mills were burned."

When news of the skirmish reached the county's settled regions, "we collected about 150 men and officers" to return to the scene and bury the dead, Balliet said. "On the 15th we took up our line of march," the officer said. "Want of ammunition prevented us from going sooner."

On September 17, "we arrived at the place of action, where we found 10 of our soldiers dead, scalped, stripped naked, and . . . tomahawked, their throats cut." The soldiers buried the bodies "and returned without even seeing any of these . . . bloody executors of British tyranny," Balliet said.

In his September letter to Reed, Colonel Rea stated, "we are nearly destitute of ammunition." He asked that the state government ". . . furnish us with . . . at least 400 or 500 weight of powder and lead."

The colonel noted that the county had previously received two shipments of ammunition: "The first quantity sent up was distributed among the frontier inhabitants, and the last given to the seven-months men," militia soldiers who had enlisted for a period of seven months.

Few attacks occurred during October and November. At Fort Wyoming, for instance, Colonel Zebulon Butler advised the Board of War on October 26 "that nothing material has happened here since my last." His soldiers had been watching for enemy war parties, but ". . . my scouting parties make no discovery of them nor their signs." As 1780 ended, settlers across the frontier began hoping that winter's approach would discourage new raids.

Then on December 7, Thomas Connelly, a 20-year-old Loyalist deserter, turned himself in at Fort Wyoming. He asserted that he had belonged to a war party "of 20 white men and five Indians who left Niagara" in mid- November.

Interrogated, Connelly readily provided information about Fort Niagara: "the number of troops of white men consists of about 600 including the rangers. The Indians are very unsteady—sometimes near 2,000 men, women and children who all draw rations."

Connelly also disclosed that "about two months ago John Montour, one of the Indian head warriors, was killed near this post by a small party that came across them from Wyoming as they was on their return from Fort Allen." The deserter appeared to be describing the September skirmish between Indians and the Northampton County militia near Nescopeck.

Among other matters, Connelly said that the war party he belonged to had raided a family named Harvey near Wyoming. "They carried away . . . six men and boys. . . . Harvey's daughter and one other girl they sent back after having them some time and leading them off a considerable distance."

Charles Miner, in his 1845 *History of Wyoming*, listed the date of the Harvey raid as December 6. He reported that Captain John Franklin took 26 Wyoming Valley men and pursued the raiding party on December 7, the same day that Connelly showed up at the fort. Franklin's force went up the North Branch, "crossing the Susquehanna . . . three miles above Tunkhannock," Miner said. Franklin eventually realized that the raiders had a substantial head start, and he returned to Fort Wyoming.

Officers at Fort Wyoming examined Connelly closely, then sent a copy of his statement downriver to Colonel Smith, the Northumberland County prothonotary at Sunbury. In turn, Smith gave details of the deserter's information to Governor Reed in a December 30 letter. One disclosure, in particular, had caused alarm at Sunbury: an Indian war captain called Thonop had left Fort Niagara around the same time that Connelly's company did. The deserter told his interrogators at Fort Wyoming that "the two parties was (sic) to have come out together, but differed in sentiments about the mode of their war. The whites determined to make prisoners, and the other savages to murder all they could, without distinction of age or sex."

Thonop's war party consisted of 30 Indians "and intended their stroke in the forks" of the Susquehanna. "They were not to make any prisoners but murder all that came in their way," Smith said.

The colonel reported that this news "alarmed the inhabitants much," partly because the information arrived at Fort Augusta "about the time the Lancaster County Militia was setting off for their respective homes," Smith said.

The raiders hadn't reached the Susquehanna confluence by the time that Smith wrote to Reed from Sunbury. "We are lately in hopes they will not be able to make their intended stroke as the river and creeks are now pretty high and driving thick with ice," Smith said. Nonetheless, "we fear they may hover on our frontier during the winter and give us an early stroke in the spring."

Chapter 17

Fort Augusta soldiers seize boats shipping flour to Wyoming

In late October 1780, soldiers at Fort Augusta startled boatmen sailing up the Susquehanna River with supplies bound for Fort Wyoming, a Connecticut outpost nearly 70 miles upriver on the North Branch. The soldiers—members of the Pennsylvania militia—stopped the vessels and confiscated their cargo.

Prior to the war, pioneers from Connecticut had streamed into what has since become northeast Pennsylvania. They organized settlements on land claimed by Connecticut on the strength of an old land grant by a 17th-century English king. Pennsylvania, of course, challenged these settlements.

Throughout the Revolutionary War, military units that operated in the Wyoming Valley were regarded as part of Connecticut's army and took their orders from Hartford, the capital of Connecticut. To be certain, the Revolution had forced this regional conflict onto a back burner, where it remained until the Pennsylvanians suddenly seized the boats at Sunbury.

"I have stopped two boats loaded with flour," Colonel Samuel Hunter advised Colonel Zebulon Butler, the Connecticut commander at Wilkes-Barre, in an October 23 letter.

The supplies were needed by the Pennsylvania militia stationed at Sunbury, Hunter explained, disclosing that his action came at the express direction of Pennsylvania's highest authority.

"Sir," Hunter told Butler, "I received instructions from His Excellency, Governor Reed, ordering me to stop, for the use of the post at Sunbury, all supplies drawn from the commissaries of the counties of Lancaster, York and Cumberland for the garrison at Wyoming . . ."

Colonel Butler quickly notified the Board of War of Hunter's action, which occurred as provisions for the Wyoming troops were running very low. "The garrison has not had either flour or meal for above 20 days, only pounded corn, and no meat more than two days in six, and that borrowed of the Inhabitants," Butler reported in an October 26 letter.

The Connecticut officer acknowledged sending troops into Pennsylvania for supplies. "Our situation respecting provision is bad enough at present," Butler said. He added that he had "had a party down the river about three weeks after flour."

The flour seized at Sunbury "was likely procured by way of some of the commissaries, but carried to a mill and packed, and brought 50 miles by soldiers I sent for that purpose."

Butler added that "with respect to bread, I expect we shall have a mill going in six days. A purchasing commissary may purchase near enough wheat at this place to supply the garrison."

Hunter's stopping of the boats breathed fresh life into an old controversy between the Wyoming Valley settlements and their downriver neighbors. King Charles II of England had created a conflict over land in the upper Susquehanna River Valley between Connecticut and Pennsylvania. In 1662, Charles granted land to the Connecticut Colony territory north of the 41st degree of latitude in what has since become Pennsylvania but was then forests and mountains inhabited by Native Americans. As it happened, the grant included the land along the Susquehanna River's North and West branches. Nineteen years later—in 1681—the same king granted land to William Penn that lay west of the Delaware River and extended north to the 42nd degree. Each colony regarded itself as the rightful claimant of the territory between the 41st and 42 degrees.

The Six Nations ceded their rights to this land as part of the New Purchase of 1768. During the late 1760s and early 1770s, Connecticut people, as well as some from Rhode Island, began traveling west across the Hudson and Delaware rivers and settling in what they regarded as western Connecticut. Pennsylvanians were also moving into the region, which Pennsylvania authorities regarded as part of their colony. Strife soon set in.

By the beginning of the American Revolutionary War, Connecticut had organized the upper North Branch Valley as Westmoreland County. In turn, Pennsylvania considered the same region as part of Northampton County. In 1772, with the creation of Northumberland County, with Sunbury as the county seat, the North Branch Valley became part of Northumberland County.

Armed conflicts broke out. Although Connecticut and Pennsylvania suspended hostilities during the Revolution, the tensions didn't dissipate. The two colonies may have transformed into states as the Revolutionary War progressed, but each regarded itself as the rightful claimant of the territory between the 41st and 42 degrees.

Governor Reed referred to the conflict when telling the Board of War why Hunter had stopped the Connecticut boats: Not only had "the measure . . . been approved unanimously in the (state's Supreme

In October 1780, Pennsylvania militia soldiers at Fort Augusta began seizing boats shipping flour up this stretch of the Susquehanna River's North Branch north of Sunbury. The boats were bound for the Wyoming Valley.

Executive) Council," but was also "pleasing to the (Pennsylvania) Assembly."

Reed asserted that the Wyoming garrison had little military value to the United States and "can only be considered as holding possession of territory disputed between this state and that of Connecticut."

He also alleged that "very great abuses . . . have been practiced at that post where provisions have been issued to settlers under the denomination of soldiers" as an encouragement "to settle" in the region.

In addition, the garrison was under "the command of Continental officers who . . . are personally interested in the land in controversy (and) taking every measure during the dispute to establish their claims and extend their settlement," Reed contended.

The governor noted that General Washington had withdrawn the Continental troops from Northumberland County. Washington, Reed said, "is too just and reasonable to expect we should wholly support a post on a frontier claimed by another state while we are left alone to defend ourselves."

Reed asserted that "the produce of the settlement at Wyoming is quite sufficient for the supply without drawing it at such a distance, but the inhabitants do not choose to furnish the garrison while it can be drawn from the counties below . . . without expense or charge to them." He contrasted conditions at Wyoming with "the distress of the post at Sunbury and its dependencies where we are obliged to have a garrison of 200 men in a country so desolate that it does not afford a subsistence to the few wretched inhabitants left there."

The commissaries who had provided flour to the Wyoming men were Pennsylvania officials, and Reed told the Board of War that "it seems reasonably expected they should supply their own state first."

The controversy over supplies hadn't been resolved by the time Colonel Butler sent an express rider from Fort Wyoming down to Fort Augusta in late November with a letter for Colonel Hunter. Butler wanted to know if the Pennsylvania officer was still stopping Connecticut boats. "We have lately received 100 head of cattle from Pennsylvania by order of Congress for the use of this post, and an order on the commissioners of Cumberland County for 40 barrels of flower and for some liquor which I expect to send for soon providing it can come, but it will be needless to send if you must stop it," Butler said.

Butler asked Hunter to send his response with Butler's messenger: "Let me know what I may depend on, as the season of the year requires haste in procuring provisions for this post."

Writing to the governor on December 2, Hunter stated that until Reed's order was countermanded, he intended to continue seizing the Wyoming boats. "It seems a little strange to me that they can be supplied with provisions at that post when we cannot get any from these counties," Hunter remarked. He asked Reed to "inform me how I shall behave in regard of these stores Col. Butler makes mention of . . ."

Hunter noted that the shipments were "ordered there by Congress."

Neither Reed nor Hunter had to wait long for new developments.

On December 14, Samuel Huntington, president of the U.S. Congress, informed Governor Reed that Congress wanted Colonel Hunter to allow the Wyoming boats to pass by Fort Augusta. Also, "to relieve the present urgent distress of the (Wilkes-Barre) garrison, it is requested that the State of Pennsylvania would order the supplies which were stopped by Lieutenant Hunter on their progress to Wyoming to be immediately forwarded to that garrison," Huntington said.

In the end, General Washington became involved. In a December 19 letter to Washington, Governor Reed explained the Pennsylvania side of the dispute. "The Inhabitants of this state do not consider (Fort Wyoming) as of Continental importance, but only as holding a possession for the state of Connecticut. . . . There are complaints of abuses in entering the settlers as soldiers and drawing rations. Every officer and soldier under Colonel Butler from Connecticut is a landholder under the Connecticut claim." Reed contended that supplying Wyoming shouldn't be a Pennsylvania responsibility. Instead, "Connecticut should support it as a state post."

The dispute spilled into the New Year. On January 26, 1781, the governor informed Hunter that Congress had "passed a resolve directing General Washington to garrison the post at Wyoming with troops of a state indifferent to the dispute subsisting between this state and Connecticut."

Washington, Reed disclosed, had ordered "a detachment of the Jersey Line under Captain Mitchell to occupy that post. We now think it our duty to revoke the order formerly given you to stay the passing provisions and supplies from this state and request you to give Captain Mitchell, who is a gentleman of fair character and a good officer, all the assistance and civility in your power."

In 1782, a Congressional commission addressed the controversy and ruled that the disputed territory belonged to Pennsylvania, not Connecticut: "We are unanimously of opinion that the State of Connecticut has no right to the lands in controversy. We are also unanimously of opinion that the jurisdiction and pre-emption of all the territory lying within the charter boundary of Pennsylvania, and now claimed by the State of Connecticut, do of right belong to the State of Pennsylvania."

Epilogue

The Pennsylvania Archives contain two letters that serve as a bridge between the events of 1780 and 1781.

The first was written by Colonel Daniel Brodhead, commander of Fort Pitt, the American outpost at Pittsburgh. The second was penned by Thomas Scott of Pennsylvania's Westmoreland County. Both were addressed to Governor Joseph Reed in Philadelphia.

In his January 22, 1781 letter to the governor, Colonel Brodhead said:

"A Grand Council of British and other savages is now holding at Detroit, and I am informed they are premeditating a descent on this post . . .

"Could a quantity of Indian goods and trinkets be procured? . . . I have never been furnished with goods of any kind, nor a penny of money to enable me to transact business with the Indians . . . The Indian captains appointed by the British commandant at Detroit are clothed in the most elegant manner, and have many valuable presents made them. The (Indian) captains I have commissioned by authority of Congress are naked, and receive nothing but a little whiskey, for which they are reviled by the Indians in general. . . . Unless a change of system is introduced, I must expect to see all Indians in favor of Britain, in spite of every address in my power."

At Westmoreland, Scott wrote to Reed on January 24:

"A few weeks will bring that season of the year when we may expect the Indians amongst us. Our condition is really deplorable. For God's sake, dear sir, interest yourself in having something done that may put an end to the present distractions of this country."

Selective Bibliography

Calloway, Colin G. *The American Revolution in Indian Country: Crisis and Diversity in Native American Communities*. New York, Cambridge University Press, 1995.

Darlington, Mary Carson. *Fort Pitt and Letters from the Frontier*. Pittsburgh. J. R. Weldin & Co. 1892

Donehoo, George P. *Indian Villages and Place Names in Pennsylvania*. Baltimore: Gateway Press Inc., 1995.

Godcharles, Frederic A. *History of Fort Freeland*. Williamsport: Lycoming Historical Society, 1922.

Graymont, Barbara. *The Iroquois in the American Revolution*. Syracuse, N.Y.: Syracuse University Press, 1972.

Hubbard, John N. *Sketches of Border Adventures in the Life and Times of Major Moses Van Campen, a Surviving Soldier of the Revolution, by his Grandson, John N. Hubbard*. Bath, NY: R. L. Underhill & Co., 1842.

Meginness, John F. *Otzinachson: A History of the West Branch Valley of the Susquehanna*. Williamsport, PA: Gazette and Bulletin Printing House, 1889.

Pennsylvania Archives, First Series. Vol. IV. Edited by Samuel Hazard. Philadelphia: Joseph Severns & Co., 1853.

———. Vol. VI. Edited by Samuel Hazard. Philadelphia: Joseph Severns & Co., 1853.

———. Vol. VII. Edited by Samuel Hazard. Philadelphia: Joseph Severns & Co., 1853.

———. Vol. VIII. Edited by Samuel Hazard. Philadelphia: Joseph Severns & Co., 1853.

Rich, Thomas P. and David W. Del Testa. *Water-powered Gristmills of Union County, Pennsylvania*. Lewisburg, Pa.: Union County Historical Society, 2013.

Seaver, James. *A Narrative of the Life of Mrs. Mary Jemison*. Canandaigua, N. Y.: J. D. Beamis and Co., 1824. (Reprint edition by Garland Publishing Inc., New York, 1977.)

Walton, William. *A Narrative of the Captivity and Sufferings of Benjamin Gilbert and His Family Who were surprised by the Indians, and taken from their Farms, on the Frontiers of Pennsylvania In the Spring, 1780*. Philadelphia: Joseph Crukshank, 1784.

Wallace, Paul A. W. *Indian Paths of Pennsylvania*. Harrisburg: Pennsylvania Historical and Museum Commission, 1971.

About the Author

JOHN L. MOORE of Northumberland is a writer and storyteller whose subjects deal with real people and actual events in Pennsylvania history.

1780: Year of Revenge is the third book in his Revolutionary Pennsylvania Series, which tells the stories of Pennsylvania and Pennsylvanians caught up in the American Revolutionary War. The volume is the author's eleventh non-fiction book. It is a companion to *Tories, Terror, and Tea* (2017), and *Scorched Earth: General Sullivan and the Senecas* (2018).

Sunbury Press Inc. published the eight non-fiction books in Moore's Frontier Pennsylvania Series in 2014.

Mr. Moore has participated in several archaeological excavations of Native American sites. These include the Village of Nain in Bethlehem, Pa.; the City Island project in Harrisburg, Pa., conducted by the Pennsylvania Historical and Museum Commission; a Bloomsburg University dig in 1999 at a Native American site near Nescopeck, Pa.; and a 1963 excavation of the New Jersey State Museum along the Delaware River north of Worthington State Forest.

Mr. Moore's 46-year newspaper career (1966-2012) included stints as a reporter for The Wall Street Journal; as managing editor of The Sentinel at Lewistown, Pa.; as editorial page editor, city editor and managing editor of The Daily Item in Sunbury, and as editor of the Eastern Pennsylvania Business Journal in Bethlehem, Pa. He was also a Harrisburg correspondent for Ottaway Newspapers in the early 1970s.

A professional storyteller, Moore specializes in historically accurate stories about Pennsylvanians. Wearing 18th century-style clothing, he often appears in the persona of Susquehanna Jack.

For information about Mr. Moore's storytelling programs and books, please contact:

John L. Moore
552 Queen Street
Northumberland, Pa. 17857
Telephone (570) 473-9803
Email: tomahawks1756@gmail.com

www.ingramcontent.com/pod-product-compliance
Lightning Source LLC
Chambersburg PA
CBHW020010050426
42450CB00005B/403